W9-ATX-722

Teaching a Lexis-Based Academic Writing Course

A Guide to
Building Academic Vocabulary

Lawrence J. Zwier

and

Gena R. Bennett

ANN ARBOR
THE UNIVERSITY OF MICHIGAN PRESS

Copyright © by the University of Michigan 2006

All rights reserved

ISBN-10: 0-472-03101-5
ISBN-13: 978-0-472-03101-6

Published in the United States of America
The University of Michigan Press

Manufactured in the United States of America

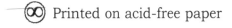 Printed on acid-free paper

2009   2008   2007   2006   4 3 2 1

Acknowledgments

Larry would like to thank Russ Werner for his excellent advice on graphics. Kelly Sippell, as usual, kept the project together through thick and thin. Thanks also go to all my students in Writing for Academic Purposes at Michigan State University, who have used *Building Academic Vocabulary* as their writing text. They gave generous feedback about the scope and sequence and the exercises, and their fondness for the metaphor activities convinced me to add them to this Teacher's Guide.

Gena would like to thank Larry Zwier for all the opportunities and guidance he's provided, as well as all her students and her husband who always inspire and motivate her.

Grateful acknowledgment is made to the following publisher for permission to reprint previously published material.

Lerner Publishing Group for "A Revolution in Healing: Biotechnology in Medicine" in *The New Biotechnology: Putting Microbes to Work* by Cynthia Gross, copyright © 1988.

Contents

Introduction

Aims of a Lexis-Based Course

Lexis-based language courses give priority to the learning of vocabulary and to the precise use of what has been learned. A lexis-based writing course concentrates on developing vocabulary that is useful in writing. Its ultimate goal is no different from that of a structure-based course, a process-based course, or any other common type of writing course: *Students should become better writers by successfully applying what they learn in class.*

A lexis-based writing course is especially appropriate for high-intermediate to advanced students. Most have already learned in their previous English language classes how to build an essay that meets the expectations of an academic audience. When asked to name the way in which they can best improve their English, such students routinely respond, "increase my vocabulary."

I think these higher-level students are right. They need more practice with grammar and organization, but they rarely need more instruction in them. Many of their apparent grammar problems are actually lexico-syntactic faults: The student either uses a vocabulary item that does not go well with other sentence elements or uses an effective item but does not know which structures or collocations should go with it. For example, a student who writes **Only a few scientists accepted to work on the development of nuclear bombs* seems to have made a grammar mistake. Remediating that sentence, however, does not require a grammatical change. Simply changing *accepted* to *agreed* would fix everything. The basic problem is that the student chose a verb that cannot have an infinitive as its direct object, <u>not</u> that the grammar of the sentence is flawed.

Theorists have difficulty determining what it means to "know" a word or phrase. The generally accepted stance is that there are many levels at which a vocabulary item can be "known." Very basic levels are predominantly *receptive*, involving simple recognition of the item and a general idea about what it means. The highest levels involve *productive* ability as well. At this level, the speaker commands the item precisely in his or her own use of the target language and might even be able to make puns or clever turns of phrase involving the item. Precise use demands a deep knowledge of what other vocabulary or grammatical structures can surround the target item. Manipulation of the item to make an effective joke requires an ability to see connections between the target item and other terms. Take, for example, a pun once made by the comic novelist Peter DeVries: "My wife's fondness for garage sales is making us baroque." Whether or not you think the joke is funny, you would probably acknowledge that anyone able to construct that pun has a deep understanding of *baroque* and sees its connection to other lexical items—notably the near-homophone *broke*.

Building Academic Vocabulary (BAV), and any writing course in which it is used, is best suited to moving an item beyond a student's receptive vocabulary and into his or her productive vocabulary. Most high-intermediate or advanced students have encountered almost all the key vocabulary before, and many of them have a relatively firm understanding of what these items mean. For example, most students at that level would be familiar with *consist of.* They have seen it in what they have read, and it poses no obstacle to their understanding. Using it in their own writing, however, is another matter altogether. To do that correctly, they have to know that its subject must be a whole thing and its object must represent all parts of the whole. The verb cannot be in a passive form (*is consisted of*) or a full-verb progressive form (*is consisting of*). The list of constraints could go on and on, all of them triggered solely by the properties of this vocabulary item.

The overall aim of a *BAV*-directed, lexis-based writing course is to make important constraints on the key vocabulary explicit, thereby making a student aware of many features that are implicit for (and perhaps not even recognized by) native speakers of North American English. A course using *BAV* gives the students ample practice in using what they have learned and places heavy emphasis on both paraphrasing and essay assignments designed to bring out the key vocabulary. Because many constraints on usage are founded in metaphor, *BAV* also notes the image(s) influencing the properties of a given lexical item. For example, *diverge* calls up the image of going in different directions after sharing a common path, an image founded in the Latin roots of the item. It does not matter whether students know anything about those Latin roots, but it does matter that they recognize the image.

A high-level student armed with this information—and given opportunities to use it—is very likely to learn a great deal in a lexis-based writing course.

Structure of *Building Academic Vocabulary*

Each of the nine chapters in *Building Academic Vocabulary (BAV)* concentrates on one area of meaning, such as "including" or "links and correlations." The areas have been chosen for their relevance to certain modes commonly taught in university-level introductory writing courses—*describing* (especially describing a system), *comparing/contrasting*, and discussing *causes and effects*.

In fact, these three general categories form the basis for three blocks of chapters in *BAV*. Chapters 1 and 2 contain key vocabulary for describing a system, object, or person. Chapters 3, 4, and 5 present vocabulary useful in writing about similarities or differences. Chapters 6 through 9 deal with causation and its often-neglected, logically distinct cousins, correlation and facilitation. Because this book is meant for students who already have considerable experience with English, the logical distinctions signaled by vocabulary items are emphasized. There is no point in learning so much about a lexical item and then employing it to make wrong-headed claims.

The key vocabulary in each chapter is divided into groups, depending on meaning or lexico-semantic properties. Each key item is introduced and grammatically classified (countable noun, complex preposition, etc.); any commonly used related forms are also noted. For example, related forms of the adjective *diverse* are *diversity* (noun) and *diversify* (verb), but (as *BAV* notes) *diversion* is not part of the family. The key item is then shown in two different contexts, each of which is accompanied by a restatement to help the students build semantic networks. A Usage Clues box (shaded) forms the heart of the lesson about each vocabulary item—notes about its implications, possible contexts, common collocates, any fixed phrases in which it appears, and so forth. Some terms for which clear mnemonic devices exist are also followed by a short section called To Help You Remember.

Each chapter contains two types of exercises. After every two or three sections, a set of Consolidation Exercises helps students work with and understand a small roster of key vocabulary. Near the end of each chapter is a larger set of Comprehensive Review Exercises to allow students to work with all the key vocabulary in the chapter. The Answer Key to *BAV* (pages 223–30) provides definite or suggested answers to all the exercises in a chapter.

At the end of each chapter is a section called Writing Projects. This contains several options for writing that could be treated in a short form (500–600 words) or in a longer paper of about 2,000 words. The scope and sequence in this teacher's guide recommends that the student write three longer, multi-draft essays in a course of about 14 weeks. This implies one essay per multi-chapter block, so that the student may choose among the proposed writing projects for all the chapters in the block. The teacher is completely free to require more or fewer major papers—whatever the teacher feels is the best workload for everyone concerned. *BAV* gives ample suggestions, any number of which could be used.

One last notable feature in each chapter is the set of additional vocabulary. These provide an optional second tier of learning. The additional terms are underlined where they occur in the text of the chapter, but they are not explained. They are pointed out for their broad academic usefulness or their cultural interest, so that students who want to add volume to their vocabularies can draw from a list of good suggestions. The student, however, will probably have to consult a good dictionary for more information about any interesting items and will have to work independently to infer usage constraints. One matching and one fill-in exercise in each chapter test the student's understanding of additional vocabulary. The teacher is free, however, to compose production-oriented exercises that encourage a deeper knowledge of these terms.

A Sample Scope and Sequence for a Lexis-Based Writing Course

- The following sequence below assumes a 14-week term with three or four instructional hours per week. In such circumstances, the material could be covered in 42 to 56 hours of instruction. The sequence of lessons can easily be compressed into a ten-week term or expanded to fill 16 weeks.

- *BAV* is an abbreviation for *Building Academic Vocabulary*.

- The material from *BAV* is divided into three blocks of increasing length. The first two blocks take up the first half of a typical college semester, and the third block takes up the second half.

- The last element in each chapter is a set of possible writing assignments. The point of doing such writing is to use the key vocabulary correctly in an academic context. For each block, the student should do only one long essay, so each block's writing assignment offers the student at least five choices of topic and approach.

- For each chapter, this teacher's guide gives one metaphor/idiom exercise and five quizzes—four about key vocabulary and one about additional vocabulary. Teachers are free to use whichever quiz best reflects their expectations for the students. Some teachers may want to use two or even three quiz options for some chapters. That is why this scope and sequence refers to "quiz(zes)."

- Most important, this scope and sequence provides only a suggested approach to the material. Teachers should feel free to customize it to suit the needs of their students.

Block 1

Describing a System/Optional Review of Essay Structure and/or the Writing Process

Time	Content	Some Activities

Weeks 1–4 (12 to 16 hours of instruction)	**BAV Chapters 1 and 2; if necessary, some review of essay structure and the writing process (see pp. 1–20 in this guide)**
	
	• Briefly, the parts of an essay (optional)
	  • Unscrambling Essay Parts exercise
	  • Choosing the best thesis statement
	• Discussion of key vocabulary in Chapter 1 (including) and Chapter 2 (excluding)
	• Metaphor/idiom discussion for each chapter
	• Discussion of additional vocabulary for one or both chapters (optional)
	
	Writing-Process Activities
	
	• Review of basics of writing process (optional)
	• Peer editing on first draft of system-description essay
	• Teacher feedback on first draft of system-description essay (via marginal comments on the paper, ideally followed by an individual or pair conference)
	• Grade on final draft of system-description essay
		• Exercises in *BAV* as appropriate for homework or in class
		• Other exercises as the teacher sees fit (composed by the teacher)
		• Quiz(zes) about *BAV* Chapter 1
		• Quiz(zes) about *BAV* Chapter 2
		
		<u>Essay:</u>
		
		One of the writing projects at the end of *BAV* Chapter 1 (p. 21) or Chapter 2 (p. 44), or an alternative essay assigned by the teacher

Block 2

Writing about Similarities or Differences (Comparison/Contrast)

Time	Content	Some Activities
Weeks 5–8 (12–16 instructional hours; additional time may be planned for a midterm exam, if necessary)	**BAV Chapters 3, 4, and 5** • Some reminders about essay structure, if necessary in light of performance on the essay in Block 1 (above) • Discussion of key vocabulary in Chapter 3 (equivalence, similarity), Chapter 4 (difference, inequality), and Chapter 5 (changes, increases, decreases) • Metaphor/idiom discussion for each chapter • Discussion of additional vocabulary for one or more chapters (optional) **Writing-Process Activitities** • Peer editing on first draft of similarities-differences essay • Teacher feedback on first draft of similarities-differences essay • Grade final draft of similarities-differences essay	• Exercises in *BAV* as appropriate for homework or in class • Other exercises as the teacher sees fit (composed by the teacher) • Quiz(zes) about *BAV* Chapter 3 • Quiz(zes) about BAV Chapter 4 • Quiz(zes) about BAV Chapter 5 Essay: One of the writing projects at the end of *BAV* Chapter 3 (p. 65), Chapter 4 (p. 91), or Chapter 5 (p. 120), or an essay assigned by the teacher

Block 3

Causes, Effects, Correlations, and Favorable or Unfavorable Factors

Time	Content	Some Activities
Weeks 9–14 (18 –24 instructional hours; additional time may be planned for a final exam, if necessary)	**BAV Chapters 6, 7, 8, and 9** • Some reminders about essay structure, if necessary, in light of performance on Block 2 essay • Discussion of the differences between causation and correlation • Discussion about multiple causes and effects • Discussion about conditions and factors that promote or hinder a process • Discussion about key vocabulary in Chapter 6 (links, correlations), Chapter 7 (cause and effect), Chapter 8 (permitting, making easier), and Chapter 9 (stopping, preventing) • Metaphor/idiom discussion for each chapter. • Discussion of additional vocabulary for one or more chapters (optional) **Writing-Process Activities** • Peer editing on first draft of cause-effect/correlation/factors essay • Teacher feedback on first draft of cause-effect/correlation/factors essay • Grade on final draft of cause-effect/correlation/factors essay	• Exercises in *BAV* as appropriate for homework or in class • Other exercises as the teacher sees fit (composed by the teacher) • Quiz(zes) about BAV Chapter 6 • Quiz(zes) about BAV Chapter 7 • Quiz(zes) about BAV Chapter 8 • Quiz(zes) about BAV Chapter 9 Essay: A cause-effect essay, a correlation essay, or an essay discussing favorable/unfavorable factors. Students are expected not to confuse causal relationships with coincidental relationships. The logical standard for the students should be set quite high. Assignment: One of the writing projects in *BAV* Chapter 6 (p. 143), Chapter 7 (p. 165), Chapter 8 (p. 187), or Chapter 9 (p. 214), or an alternative essay assigned by the teacher

Unit 1

Fundamentals: A Reminder

The Essay and Its Parts

Most students using *Building Academic Vocabulary (BAV)* have already studied the basics of English essay structure. They do not need to hear much more about thesis statements, topic sentences, or the (not-found-in-nature) five-paragraph essay. They probably still need to practice producing them, and their writing assignments in *BAV* will give them that opportunity. To succeed in these assignments, some students may need reminders of (but not elaborate lessons about) the essay-structure principles they have already learned.

This chapter offers such a review of a few essay-structure basics. This short recap does not require a lot of instructional time. Most of it could be delivered in a single class period or, better yet, in conferences with any students who seem to need it.

Key Terms

- title
- introduction
- thesis statement
- body paragraphs
- topic sentences
- support sentences
- conclusion
- cohesive devices

1

Explanations of Some Key Terms

Thesis Statement

- Tells what the piece of writing is about (overall).

- Usually—but not always—comes at or near the end of the introduction. If the introduction is more than one paragraph long, the thesis statement might not be near the end of the first paragraph.

- Sometimes the thesis statement is made up of two or three sentences, not just one.

- Some pieces of writing have no clear thesis statement.

Topic Sentence

- States what a paragraph is about.

- Often—but not always—comes near the beginning of a paragraph. Notice in the passage "Fear of Spiders" (on pages 3–5) that it is not unusual for a topic sentence to be the second or third sentence of a paragraph.

- If a paragraph is meant to argue against a commonly held belief, the topic sentence probably comes in the middle of the paragraph, after a statement of the belief the writer considers untrue.

- Sometimes the topic is stated in more than one sentence.

- Some paragraphs have no clear topic sentence.

Supporting Ideas

- Show why the main idea of an essay or paragraph is true.

- Some common kinds of support include:
  - statistics
  - verifiable events or conditions
  - comments by respected, knowledgeable persons
  - logical reasons
  - personal anecdotes (considered weak in academic writing)

Support Sentences

These give a further explanation or examples to clarify a supporting detail.

A Sample Essay, with Key Parts Labeled

Essay	Parts
Fear of Spiders	*Title*
A strong fear of spiders is extremely common among humans. This fear, although it extends even to harmless species, is not entirely unrealistic (unless it becomes so strong that it becomes *arachnophobia*—an irrational fear that prevents someone from living a normal life). Venomous types of spider can be very dangerous indeed.	*Introduction* *Thesis Statement*
A human is far too large to be a practical source of food for any arachnid, so what purpose does a spider bite serve? A spider probably bites humans only if it feels threatened somehow. In a majority of spider-bite cases, a person does not even see the spider before it bites (and perhaps not even then), but the spider does not know that. A sleeping person, for example, may frighten a spider just by rolling near it. In a few other cases, a person notices the spider in its web (or wherever else it may live) and approaches just to have a closer look. The spider then moves, faster than the person imagined possible, toward a hand or a leg and delivers a defensive bite to protect its lair. The human perspective is that the spider is the aggressor, but the spider probably sees things differently.	*First body paragraph* *Topic Sentence 1 (2nd sentence of this paragraph)* *Supporting Detail 1.1* *Support Sentence (example) for Detail 1.1* *Supporting Detail 1.2* *Support Sentence for Detail 1.2*
Spider venom is a destroyer of living tissue. When a spider bites an insect (or another spider) it intends to eat, the venom first immobilizes the victim and then liquefies its solid organs. The spider then uses a tube-like mouth	*Topic Sentence 2* *Supporting Detail 2.1*

structure to suck up the nutrient-rich goo. When injected into a human, the venom has a similar effect, only slower ———— *Supporting Detail 2.2* and not as thorough. Parts of the skin and some muscle may be deadened by its chemical action. The strongest *Supporting Sentences* venoms are powerful enough to reach and kill nerve *for Detail 2.2* cells, most tragically those in the spinal cord and brain.

The strength of the venom depends on the species. The ——— *Topic Sentence 3* most poisonous in the world is Australia's funnel-web spider, whose venom disables a person within about 20 ——— *Supporting Detail 3.1* minutes. Almost every victim of a funnel-web bite dies ——— *Supporting Sentence* within 24 hours. In the United States, the black widow *for Detail 3.1* and the brown recluse are the main threat to humans, mostly because these types of spider often live in or near *Supporting Detail 3.2* houses and humans encounter them more frequently than they do other spiders. Both can cause significant pain and some tissue damage in humans, but their bites ——— *Supporting Sentence* are usually fatal only to very weak victims or those with *for Detail 3.2* allergies to the venom.

The most effective treatment for spider bites is an ——— *Lead-in to Topic Sentence* injection of medicine that neutralizes venom, but this only works when the victim can identify the kind of spider that delivered the bite. This is surprisingly rare. ——— *Topic Sentence 4 (3rd* Some bites are not noticed until hours afterward, by *sentence of this paragraph)* which time the spider is long gone. Even when someone ——— *Supporting Detail 4.1* notices a bite immediately, the spider often hurries away ——— *Supporting Detail 4.2* too fast to be seen clearly, if at all. In only a few cases does the victim catch or kill the spider so its species can ——— *Supporting Detail 4.3* be determined.

The uncertainty over which spider has caused a certain ——— *Topic Sentence 5* bite is so great that some species cannot be definitively said to be dangerously venomous. The hobo spider, for ——— *Supporting Detail 5.1* instance, may or may not be highly venomous. Its original home range is in Europe, where no victim of its *Supporting Sentences* bite is known to have suffered serious harm. In North *for Detail 5.1* America, the spider established itself in the Pacific Northwest some time in the first half of the 20th century.

Several near-fatal spider bites—and a few deaths—in this region have been blamed on the hobo. Scientific tests of its venom, however, have been inconsistent. Some have discovered truly harmful agents in it, and some have not. The spider's history in Europe may suggest harmlessness or may just suggest that the European hobo bites fewer humans. Some have suggested that the harmful North American bites are really from a brown recluse. The problem with this theory is that brown recluses are not known to live so far north.

Supporting Sentences for Detail 5.1 (cont.)

Aside from E.B. White's *Charlotte's Web*, very few tales in any culture have good things to say about spiders. On the contrary, cultural traditions are likely to reinforce any natural wariness about spiders. The chilly relationship between humans and arachnids is also reinforced by almost any contact between the two. A human-spider encounter usually brings pain and suffering to at least one of them.

Conclusion

Some Advice about Essay Structure

1. The labels for the passage "Fear of Spiders" show a common arrangement of essay parts. This is not the only possible way to build a piece of academic writing, but it is very clear and easy.

2. Most paragraphs should be relatively short—five to eight sentences. If you write a paragraph much longer than eight sentences, consider splitting the long paragraph into two smaller ones.

3. Certain "build-up sentences" in the introduction are supposed to do two things:

   a. lead readers' thoughts toward the main idea of the essay

   b. encourage readers to keep reading the essay

Therefore, your introduction should be somewhat entertaining, but it should be very closely related to your thesis.

> *WARNING:* Many students make a mistake by starting their introductions too generally ("In today's world, we have many problems. . . .").
>
> *WARNING:* Many students write introductions that are too long in relation to the rest of the essay—often constituting as much as 25 percent of the entire essay. The introduction should not be so long. An easy rule is to make sure your introduction is no longer than your longest body paragraph.
>
> *ADVICE:* Some students find it easier to leave some empty space for the introduction until after they have written their support paragraphs. They write the body of the essay first, and then they find a nice way to lead into it.

4. Each body paragraph in your essay should have a clear reltionship to your thesis, to paragraphs just before and just after it, and among its sentences. The language tools that tie ideas together are called cohesive devices. A few of the cohesive devices in the passage "Fear of Spiders" are:

   a. *this fear* (introductory paragraph; connects Sentences 1 and 2)

   b. *any arachnid* (Body Paragraph 1; ties in with *spider* and *arachnophobia* in Paragraph 1)

   c. *for example* (Body Paragraph 1; connects to previous sentence)

   d. Every mention of *spider venom* throughout the passage ties in with the thesis statement at the end of the introductory paragraph.

5. The concluding paragraph is the least important part of your essay. It should be merely a polite way of saying goodbye to your reader. Conclusions should be short and should contain no new information. In an essay of fewer than 1,000 words, the conclusion should not summarize or restate the main points of the essay. The reader almost certainly remembers the main points of such a short essay without a summary. Better techniques are: (1) looking to the future, (2) drawing an implication from your earlier points, and (3) making a clever observation based on your earlier points.

Exercise: Unscrambling Essay Parts

To the teacher:

1. Divide the class into groups of three or four students.

2. For each group, cut up a copy of the reading (at marked cut points) on pages 9–10. Put each set of slips into an envelope.

3. Give each group an envelope, a glue stick, and three sheets of colored paper onto which they can stick the parts. Glue-stick adhesive does not dry very fast, so the students can change their minds and try different arrangements.

4. Each group meets with another group. The groups compare their arrangements. Are there any points of disagreement?

5. Either give each student a copy of the whole reading (which will require extra photo-copying) or show the class a whole reading on an overhead transparency. Each group compares its arrangement with the original.

6. As an optional homework follow-on, each student can identify essay parts in this reading. (See the worksheet following the reading on page 11.)

Hormone Production

- -

Endocrine disorders (malfunctions of the human hormone-producing mechanisms) can have serious consequences. Hormones, like insulin or human growth hormone, are crucial physical messengers, regulating and coordinating such functions as digestion and the balance of serum minerals. Severe shortages of hormones can mean a virtual shutdown of essential bodily processes.

- -

Endocrine disorders are routinely treated by administering hormones obtained from sources outside the body of the person suffering the disorder. The supply of such chemicals in nature, however, is far short of that needed in modern medicine. Since hormones are proteins, they are perfect candidates for production by genetically engineered bacteria. This production represents one of the most useful and widespread applications of rDNA (recombinant DNA) technology.

- -

More than 5 million people worldwide take the hormone *insulin* each day to control some form of diabetes. Most of the insulin sold comes from cow or pig pancreases collected at abattoirs as a byproduct of meat production. While insulin from these sources is generally safe, it has slight structural differences from the human form. Rather than slipping comfortably past the immune defenses of the recipient, these insulin molecules are easily recognized as outsiders. Consequently, a few people taking bovine or porcine insulin develop allergic reactions as their immune systems reject the foreign intrusion. This problem is avoided by substituting human insulin, which, to be available in significant quantities, must be manufactured by genetically altered bacteria.

- -

Insulin was the first therapeutic rDNA product approved by the FDA for sale in the United States. It went on the market in 1982 under the brand name Humulin®. The development work had been done by the pioneering biotech firm Genentech; Eli Lilly and Company produced and marketed Humulin®.

- -

The biotechnology used in making insulin is more complicated that than used in making human growth hormone. The insulin molecule is made up of two polypeptide chains (linked strings of amino acids), which join to make the active form of insulin. In the production of genetically engineered insulin, the DNA that codes for the A chain is introduced into one batch of *E. coli* bacteria and the DNA for the B chain into a different one. The bacterial cells are induced to make the two chains, which are then collected, mixed, and chemically treated to make them link. The resulting insulin molecules are identical to those secreted by the human pancreas.

- -

Human growth hormone (hGH) was another early target of rDNA approaches to hormone deficiency. HGH controls the growth of bones and regulates weight gain. In some children, the pituitary gland fails to produce enough hGH for normal development, and this is evidenced by markedly short stature (perhaps only 60%–70% of normal height for a given age) and other growth deficiencies. The condition can be ameliorated, but only if hormone supplementation takes place during the growth years of childhood. Beyond this critical period, many bones (such as the femur) lose their ability to elongate.

- -

Early in the development of hGH therapy, the only sources of the hormone were the pituitary glands of human cadavers. Suppliers and marketers worried that drawing a chemical from the glands of the dead might eventually create a public relations problem. But a more serious problem was that the source was not prolific enough. First of all, the number of cadavers from which the pituitary gland could be harvested was very limited and not easily increased (within the bounds of the law). Secondly, each cadaver yielded a very small amount of the hormone—only about 4 mg, whereas one week's treatment for an individual deficient in hGH requires about 7 mg. No successful animal sources were found. Clearly, new sources were needed.

- -

The supply of human growth hormone is maintained by applying rDNA techniques and achieving high-volume synthesis. A gene for hGH production is spliced into *E. coli*, which are cultured and exploited in very large amounts. A 500-liter tank of bacterial culture can produce as much hGH as could have been derived from 35,000 cadavers. Growth hormone produced by this technique was approved for human use in 1985 and is now commonplace.

- -

Source: Adapted from Cynthia S. Gross, *The New Biotechnology: Putting Microbes to Work* (Minneapolis: Lerner, 1988).

Worksheet 1

In the reading "Hormone Production," find and label as many of the following as you can. You can write your labels (and do any highlighting) on your group's pasted-together copy of the reading.

Introduction Paragraph(s) (Label it/them.)

Thesis Statement (Draw a circle around it.)

Topic Sentences (Draw a box around each one.)

Supporting Ideas Related to Each Topic Sentence (Underline them.)

Concluding Paragraph (Label it.)

Cohesive Devices (Highlight them with a colored marker.)

Exercise: Choosing the Best Thesis Statement

Review page 21 in *Building Academic Vocabulary*, Writing Project #2. Here are some sentences people might try to use as a thesis statement for an essay about this question. Which ones are the best, and why?

1. According to *Webster's Ninth New Collegiate Dictionary*, a family is "a group of individuals living under one roof and usually under one head."

2. Throughout the world, there are many different kinds of families, so it is impossible to say exactly what a family is.

3. Everyone has a family.

4. Society is most stable if we conceive of the family as a married couple and their children, if any.

5. In order to meet the needs of the sick, the poor, and other unfortunates, it is best to think of the family as an extended group involving three or four generations—from great-grandparents to young children.

6. The concept of the family is very useful for making us responsible and loving people.

7. I have succeeded only because I got constant support from my family.

Exercise: Topic Sentences

Following Paragraphs 1–3 are four sentences. Circle the letter of the best sentence to fill in the blank in each paragraph. In Paragraphs 4 and 5 on pages 16 and 17, fill in the blanks with an effective topic clause (4) or sentence in your own words.

1. _____

   _____.

   One clear element in it is that the first patent for what we now call a laser was issued (in 1960) to Charles Townes and Arthur Schawlow, who based their patent application on work they had done at Bell Laboratories. Beyond that, things get murkier. Townes and Schawlow had published about the principles of the technology as early as 1958. Gordon Gould claimed to have come up with the idea of a laser (and to have written notes about it) as early as 1957, but he didn't file for a patent until 1959. In any case, Gould gets credit for coining the word laser (from "light amplification by stimulated emission of radiation"), and the U.S. Patent Office eventually granted him a laser-related patent in the late 1970s. A third important character in the story is Theodore Maiman, who, in 1960, built a working optical laser (one involving visible light)— probably the first functional laser.

   Which of the following would be the best topic sentence for this paragraph? Be prepared to explain why.

   a. The history of the laser shows clearly who should get credit for the invention.

   b. Early ideas for the laser were very different from ideas that came later.

   c. The invention of the laser makes for a somewhat unclear chapter in technological history.

   d. No invention has inspired more lawsuits than the laser.

2. _____

    _____.

If two cultures share a distinctive burial style or fishing method, the members of one culture are assumed to have learned it by meeting and observing the members of the other. Diffusionists run the gamut from the extreme to the mild. The former, such as G. Elliot Smith, posit very few centers from which cultural features radiate. In Smith's characterization, there was only one such center—ancient Egypt—for all advanced cultural achievements, such as writing. Less extreme diffusionists include well-known anthropologists of the early to middle 20th century such as Franz Boas and R. H. Lowie. Their approach, while emphasizing the importance of contact among cultures, allowed for individual invention as well. In other words, if two cultures shared a burial style or a peculiar fishing method, one might have borrowed it from the other or each might have come up with the idea on its own. Nor did this mild viewpoint restrict the center of diffusion to one place. Several centers might have functioned simultaneously to spread cultural features, much as a handful of pebbles thrown into a pond will create several ripple patterns radiating from several centers.

Which of the following would be the best topic sentence for this paragraph? Be prepared to explain why.

a. Since the 19th century, cultural diffusionists have explained shared features among various cultures in terms of a process of contact and borrowing.

b. Since the 19th century, cultural diffusionists have been excluded from the mainstream of anthropology.

c. Since the 19th century, cultural diffusionists have insisted that all cultural achievements originated in one place.

d. Since the 19th century, cultural diffusionists have tried very hard to spread the best aspects of civilization throughout the world.

3. _____

_____.

Superconductivity depends on critical points—of temperature, current density, and magnetic field strength—where sudden changes occur. This became clear long ago, when Heike Kamerlingh Onnes (Nobel laureate in physics, 1913) first achieved virtually zero electrical resistance in a mercury wire cooled to 4.2 K and named the state of the metal "superconductivity." As far as we know, not every material can become superconductive, but any material that can do so has its own Critical Temperature (T_c). For pure metals, this is typically very low, under 20 K. For many newly developed ceramics, T_c is much higher—near or even above 100 K. Critical Current Density (J_c) refers to the fact that, at a given temperature, a material can carry only so much electrical current and stay superconductive. If the current density exceeds J_c the material will suddenly lose its near-zero resistance and flip to its normal resistive state. Most complex of all is the third factor, Critical Magnetic Field (H_c), which refers to the strength of the magnetic field around the superconductor. Superconductors have a unique ability to prevent an external magnetic field from penetrating the superconductive material—up to H_c. In one kind, called type I or "soft" superconductors. The material reverts to its normal resistive state if the external magnetic field reaches or surpasses H_c.

What would be the best topic sentence for this paragraph? Be prepared to say why.

a. In considering superconductivity, our normal sense of physical change as gradual has to be set aside. Superconductivity depends on critical points—of temperature, current density, and magnetic field strength—where sudden changes occur.

b. Advances in superconductivity research have led to the development of new materials that have reshaped modern industry. It represents the vital role played by materials science in modern society.

c. Superconductivity requires certain conditions of temperature, current density, and magnetic field strength. These create important changes in the arrangement of molecules within a material.

d. Maintaining a superconductive state in a given material is a difficult and expensive process. This alone justifies the high level of grant funding for research in this area.

4. By 1960, when Stanley Kramer's *Inherit the Wind* was released, the issues central to the Scopes "Monkey Trial" of 1925 (which the film fictionally portrayed) had become slightly quaint, at least for mainstream U.S. society. The general outlook for real science at school was somewhat brighter in those days. Kramer could get away with sympathetically portraying evolutionism as progressive and with lampooning Bible-toting creationists. It's an open question whether a film with that point of view—and with such unflattering characterizations of creationists—could long endure in today's film market. It should amaze us that the basic issue is still with us: Should public schools teach evolution as scientific fact or should religion-based views be presented as equally possible? We have been debating this for at least eight decades. By now, evolution should have killed off its rivals, and schoolkids throughout the land should be examining the fossil evidence. But creationists, many of them disingenuously traveling under the name of "intelligent-design advocates," are perhaps more powerful in the United States than ever before. Their influence has reached into the White House and Congress. Many avowed creationists head federal agencies. If an updated *Inherit the Wind* were released today, it might still be nominated for four Academy Awards as the original was in 1960, but _____

_____.

In this paragraph, the topic sentence comes at the end. Complete the last sentence. Write your answer on the lines.

5. _____

_____.

Much attention has focused on a period from 1645 to 1715, known as the Maunder minimum (named for E. W. Maunder, a late 19th-century astronomer), when sunspot activity was virtually nil. For some time, researchers wondered whether this period of marked inactivity might simply have been a period of poor record-keeping. That issue seems settled, and most historical astronomers accept that reliable observers were watching the sun regularly and that a remarkable paucity of sunspots truly did characterize this long period. The years of the Maunder minimum correspond to tree-ring evidence of higher-than-normal concentrations of carbon 14, which would be consistent with a period of very little solar flaring. Evidence from the late 17th century also reveals a period of colder-than-average global temperatures. This has thrust the issue of solar variability into one of the most intense debates of the 21st century, the contest over the extent and causes of global warming.

Compose a good topic sentence for the paragraph. Write your answer on the lines.

Writing Processes

Key Terms

- topic
- approach
- planning
- narrowing
- writing
- revising
- cutting
- pasting

Explanation of Some Key Terms

Topic—the subject area that a statement, paragraph, or entire piece of writing is about.

Narrowing—finding a more focused, easier-to-handle aspect of a topic. Assignments often state topics very generally to allow the students to choose an interesting sub-topic. Teachers are also interested in seeing how well a student can adjust the topic to the length of the essay and to the interests of potential readers.

Revising—in U.S. English, the process of making changes to a piece of writing after it has been completed.

Cutting and Pasting—functions in writing while using a computer. Cutting involves removing part of a passage. Pasting involves inserting them into another part. These functions are easy to perform with a computer, but they have led to errors that are not common in handwritten or typed pieces of writing. A cut-and-paste error results in a sequence of sentences that don't fit together well.

Writing Processes and a Lexis-Based Course

Despite frequent reference to "the writing process" by writing teachers, it is worth remembering that there is not just one process used by fluent writers of English. Anyone who spends considerable time among professional writers can attest that different writers follow different processes. That is why this guide uses the term *writing processes.*

Since process-based writing courses became popular in the 1970s, the writing world has changed a great deal, largely because of computer-related capabilities now available to most university students. Consequently, much of what was once said about nearly every stage in any author's writing process now sounds quaint. The planning stage has been transformed by sophisticated Internet search engines. The writing and revising stages now blend, separate, and blend again, as students freely cut, paste, and respond to grammar-check and spell-check feedback from their word-processing software. A ramped-up kind of recursiveness has been introduced into the writing stage.

Whereas many writing courses are called "process-oriented," most of them are not really. I have yet to meet a writing teacher who was dismissive of writing products. If pressed, most teachers would admit that a student's adherence to "the process" counts for little if he or she consistently turns in dismal products. This is only fair. Sensible teachers strike a reasonable balance between process and product. The process is important because it encourages independence and a portability of skills. The product is important because writers in the real world are almost always judged by what they produce, not (except in cases of plagiarism) by how they produce it.

Bearing in mind the multi-various nature of writing processes, it is still worth giving an outline of the stages most commonly recognized as fitting, somehow and in some sequence, into whatever process a writer goes through:

1. Pre-writing

    a. choosing a topic

    b. narrowing the topic

    c. planning

2. Writing

    a. choosing and verifying content

    b. organizing content

    c. choosing effective lexical items and syntactic arrangements

3. Revising

    a. getting feedback from readers on one or two early drafts

    b. changing the content and organization to reflect the most perceptive points in the feedback

    c. adjusting lexis and syntax in light of the feedback and changes in content

    d. producing a final draft

A few elements of this outline are worth emphasizing. The most important in a classroom is the feedback part of the revising stage. Peer editing (getting feedback from several other students) should occur after every early draft of the major papers in a lexis-based course. This is the main reason for writers to meet with you as a class instead of just sending things to you by e-mail. Normally, peer editing is directed toward issues of content and organization, since the students are assumed to lack expertise in issues of grammar and vocabulary. In a lexis-based course, however, it useful to allow comments about lexis, especially about the use of key words in *BAV*. Writers should adjust their lexis to use as many key words as possible and to use them correctly.

Unit 2

BLOCK 1

Describing a System, Object, or Person (*BAV* Chapters 1 and 2)

Chapter 1: Including, Making Up

Thinking about Metaphors

Fill in the middle column with the concepts that, in your native language, fit each description in the left-hand column. Write in your native language, if necessary, and then translate into English. In the right-hand column, write any concepts that you know of that, in English usage, fit each description at the left. Some concepts have been supplied to help you get started.

	In My Native Language	In English
Things that can contain other things, like a box contains the things inside it		*a nation* *a poem*

Things (besides physical objects) that have many pieces		a philosophical system
Things that can get you "wrapped up" in them		studies a job
Things that can reach around other things, as if encircling them		borders of a country the limits of a group

Chapter 1: Including, Making Up

Additional Vocabulary Quiz

I. Categorizing

Cross out the one item in each set that—*in its meaning as used in Chapter 1*—fits most poorly into the category. Be prepared to give reasons for your choice if your teacher asks you to.

> **Example:**
>
> Making schedules: ~~clock~~   calendar   appointment
>
> <u>Note</u>: *Clock* is not totally unrelated to the category, but the other two terms relate more strongly.

Vocabulary related to:

1. **Being exact:**	superficial	meticulous	accurate
2. **Sex:**	sexually explicit	autopsy	reproductive system
3. **Money:**	compass	budget	currency
4. **Groups of people:**	string quartet	nuclear family	shores
5. **Things that make you feel better:**	massage	therapy	arthritis

II. Paraphrasing

Use the best item from the list to rephrase each statement. Change the form of the item if necessary to fit the grammar of the sentence. You may also change words in the sentence itself. Do not change the meaning of the original item. Use each item from the list only once.

access	nucleus
commute	time-consuming
measure	

1. E-mail is great because it cuts down on conversations that go on way too long.

   _____

   _____

2. On the average, a person in the Twin Cities metro area spends 45 minutes driving to work and 45 minutes driving back home.

   _____

   _____

3. Only four people can get into the safe, because they're the only ones who know the combination.

   _____

   _____

4. The central planning board of the Green Environment Movement is in Houston, Texas.

   _____

   _____

5. Planes fly into the center of a hurricane to take exact readings of wind speed and air pressure.

_____

_____

III. Summarizing

Using at least five additional vocabulary words from Chapter 1 (see page 217 of *BAV*), summarize the information given in the chart. Your summary should be a full, well-connected paragraph. Underline the words you use from Chapter 3.

Average One-Way Commuting Time to Work for Selected U.S. Cities in 2000 (in minutes)

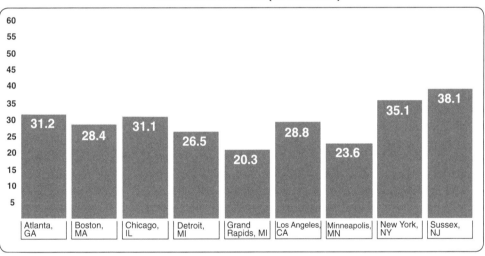

Atlanta, GA	Boston, MA	Chicago, IL	Detroit, MI	Grand Rapids, MI	Los Angeles, CA	Minneapolis, MN	New York, NY	Sussex, NJ
31.2	28.4	31.1	26.5	20.3	28.8	23.6	35.1	38.1

Source: Arbitron, Inc. "Average Travel Time to Work Comparison in Minutes for all Markets," 2004.
www.arbitron.com/national_radio/travel_result.asp

Chapter 1: Including, Making Up

Quiz 1

I. Fill in the Blanks

Fill in each blank with the best item from the list. Change the form of the item if necessary to fit the grammar of the sentence. Some items on the list will not be used.

all told	contain	made of
composed	encompass	made up of
constitute	involve	

1. _____, 15 computer servers controlled the lighting during the Super Bowl.

2. Eastern Europe is _____ Russia and the former Soviet or communist republics that used to be under its power.

3. Rafting down the Yellowstone River in May _____ negotiating many tricky passages like the rocks at Tom Miner Creek.

4. As simple as its plot seems, *Camelot* _____ some rather hard-hitting and thoughtful dialogue about the nature of power.

5. Several small, perfectly timed releases of nanobots _____ Professor Johnson's experiments.

II. Paraphrasing

Use the best item from the list to rephrase each statement. Change the form of the item if necessary to fit the grammar of the sentence. You may also change words in the sentence itself. Do not change the meaning of the original statement. Use each item from the list only once.

be composed of	involve
consist of	mainstream
encompass	

1. The most important scientific theories started out as ideas that most people considered strange.

   _____

   _____

2. The Oort Cloud, an area of space just outside our solar system, has a relatively dense center and an immense region of widely dispersed icy particles.

   _____

   _____

3. Technically, the term *the tropics* covers any location between 23° north latitude and 23° south latitude.

   _____

   _____

4. Most tree trunks have several rings of woody xylem on the inside surrounded by a layer of phloem, including the bark, on the outside.

   _____

   _____

5. Becoming a licensed psychiatrist is not easy, because you have to complete medical school and get a psychology degree.

_____

_____

III. Applying the Vocabulary

Using at least five words from Chapter 1, summarize the information given. Your summary should be a full, well-connected paragraph about 100 words long. Underline the words you use from Chapter 1.

Some Common Foods Widely Rejected Before Becoming Internationally Popular

Food	Place of Origin	Rejected Elsewhere Because
Tomato	Andes Mountains, South America	Belongs to the nightshade family (which also contains some poisonous plants); stems and leaves have strong odor
Potato	Andes Mountains, South America	Unattractive shape and color; green spots in uncooked potatoes can be poisonous
Hot Peppers (chili peppers)	The Americas, especially the Caribbean	Some varieties are painfully hot if not processed properly; after handling peppers one may experience burning of the eyes, skin, nose, etc.
Durian	Southeast Asia	Strong smell that lingers in houses; large, potentially harmful spikes on outside of fruit
Seaweed	Worldwide	Strong smell, unpleasant texture

Chapter 1: Including, Making Up

Quiz 2

I. Sentence Completion

Circle the best item to complete each sentence. Be careful. In some sentences both choices might be possible, but one is a better choice than the other.

1. After a *(mainstream/comprehensive)* examination of the building, the inspector declared that it was safe.

2. Several unions dominated by Italian and Irish workers decided to *(form/make up)* a labor coalition in North Jersey.

3. The Campus Youth League, despite its name, *(comprises/constitutes)* people of all ages who are interested in its public service projects.

4. Pressed concrete and steel reinforcing bars *(make up/are involved in)* the walls of the Walker Tower.

5. St. Paul's Winter Carnival *(encompasses/contains)* 96 separate events in a variety of locations throughout Ramsey County.

II. Paraphrasing

Use the best item from the list to rephrase each statement. Change the form of the item if necessary to fit the grammar of the sentence. You may also change words in the sentence itself. Do not change the meaning of the original statement. Use each item from the list only once.

be composed of	include
contain	involve
encompass	

1. Currently, the U.S. military has only volunteers in its ranks. There are no draftees at this time.

   _____

   _____

2. The agricultural approach known as the Green Revolution embraced a variety of techniques, from the development of hardier seeds to more efficient ways of plowing the soil.

   _____

   _____

3. If we want to avoid unpleasant confrontations, we should make sure that Gordon and Pete are not both invited to the party.

   _____

   _____

4. To get a scholarship to Charles University, you have to fill out two application forms, write an essay, present a portfolio of your achievements, and speak personally with four or five administrators.

_____

_____

5. A time capsule is a sealed box or tube, inside of which are items common in everyday life at the time the capsule is filled.

_____

_____

III. Applying the Vocabulary

Using at least five words from Chapter 1, summarize the information given. Your summary should be a full, well-connected paragraph. Underline the words you use from Chapter 1.

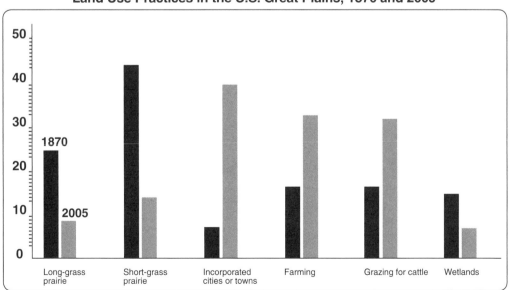

Land Use Practices in the U.S. Great Plains, 1870 and 2005

Note: The *Great Plains* refers to all or part of Colorado, Kansas, Montana, Nebraska, North Dakota, Oklahoma, South Dakota, and Texas.
Note: Figures do not add up to 100 because uses may overlap.
Figures are for exercise purposes only. Not drawn from actual data.

Chapter 1: Including, Making Up

Quiz 3: Collocations and Common Phrases

I. Collocations and Common Phrases

Fill in each blank with the best item from the list. Not every item on the list will be used. Some items may be used more than once.

a wide range	explosion	naturally
are	from	of
bomb	into	to
dangerous attempts	investigation	total
decided to		

1. The category "ungulates" (hoofed animals) encompasses _____ animals, from elephants to aardvarks.

2. A truly comprehensive _____ of government wrongdoing should look into actions by people at every level, from the top down.

3. A _____ of four main layers—the crust, the mantle, the outer core, and the inner core—make up our planet.

4. To counter the school board's plan, people in our neighborhood _____ form a group called Neighbors Opposed (NO).

5. Rescuing the lost hikers involved many _____ to descend into the cavern where they were trapped.

6. A "dirty _____" is a device that contains harmful radioactive materials meant to disperse over a wide area when it blows up.

7. Although birds are probably related to the long-vanished dinosaurs, most palaeo-biologists do not claim that any dinosaur actually evolved _____ a bird.

8. Experimental poets and writers, like Billy Lee Trask and Ioanna Darescu, were drawn to New Orleans, where they could be themselves without paying any attention to the mainstream _____ American literary life.

II. Paraphrasing

Using the item in parentheses, rephrase each statement. Change the form of the item if necessary to fit the grammar of the sentence. You may also change words in the sentence itself. Do not change the meaning of the original statement.

1. *(comprise)* There were five seasons in the calendar of the Akrubian people: the dry cold, the wet cold, the planting time, the heat, and the harvest.

   _____

   _____

2. *(make up)* The divisions of the Accounting Department are: accounts receivable, accounts payable, tax accounting, and the general ledger.

   _____

   _____

3. *(all told)* If you include students on our bowling team, table tennis team, and cheerleading squad, a total of 213 students at Ford High School play some sort of varsity sport.

   _____

   _____

4. *(consist of)* Usually, the term *Antarctica* is used to mean not only the continental land-mass but also the nearby ice shelves, ice-filled seas, and islands south of about 70° south latitude.

_____

_____

5. *(be composed of)* The public transit system in the Twin Cities is a network of bus routes and one new light-rail line from downtown Minneapolis to the airport.

_____

_____

III. Applying the Vocabulary

Using at least five words from Chapter 1, summarize the reading passage "Taxonomy" (see Appendix 1, pages 191–92). A beginning sentence for the summary has been written for you, to help you get started. Use your own words. Underline the words you use from Chapter 1.

Summary

Crucial similarities among living beings determine how scientists group them with other creatures.

Chapter 1: Including, Making Up

Quiz 4: Key Words and Related Word Forms

I. Fill in the Blanks

Fill in each blank with the best item from the list. Use each word only once.

compass	contents
component	evolution
content	

1. In this course, we will study the _____ of early Rome from a locally powerful republic into a dynamic empire.

2. As we turned around in a slow circle, six smoking volcanoes stood within the _____ of our vision. Who knew how many more might be behind them?

3. The most important _____ of any armed force is not the general or the common soldier but the mid-level officer, the first or second lieutenant whose personality determines the character of the unit.

4. This book is cleverly written, but ultimately it doesn't really say anything. I can't recommend it because it has so little real _____.

5. By the time modern archaeologists reached most of the burial places, the _____ of the jars and treasure chests inside had been carried off by grave-robbers.

II. Paraphrasing

Use the best item from the list to rephrase each statement. Change the form of the item if necessary to fit the grammar of the sentence. You may also change words in the sentence itself. Do not change the meaning of the original statement. Use each word or phrase from the list only once.

comprehensive treatment	teller
consists primarily of	Theory of Evolution
inclusive	

1. The bank employee at the window carefully counted my money and confirmed that I was depositing $750.

   _____

   _____

2. Many people are surprised to learn that the most prevalent gas in Earth's atmosphere is nitrogen.

   _____

   _____

3. To get an A on your term paper, you can't just state the obvious or easy-to-find aspects of your topic. You have to consider every aspect fairly and weigh its importance.

   _____

   _____

4. Actually, Charles Darwin espoused a Theory of Natural Selection. Later interpreters started calling it by another name, which is inaccurate and tends to anger many conservatives.

   _____

   _____

5. I'm opposed to allowing only juniors or seniors to join the chess club. We use school facilities for our meetings, so I think we should open the club to all students at the school.

   _____

   _____

III. Applying the Vocabulary

Using at least five words from Chapter 1, summarize the information illustrated. Your answer should be a full, well-connected paragraph about 100 words long. Underline the words you use from Chapter 1.

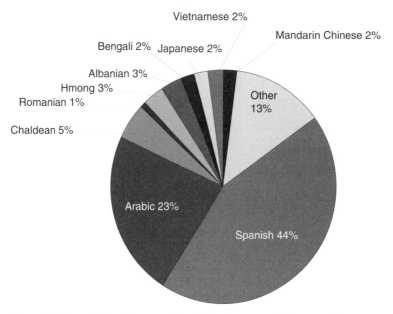

Michigan's Most Commonly Spoken Languages Other than English, 2000–2001

Source: Michigan Office of Language Acquisition, Language Enhancement, and Academic Achievement for Limited English Proficiency Students, citing the U.S. Dept. of Education, 2002.

Chapter 2 : Excluding, Not Being Part Of

Thinking about Metaphors

Fill in the middle column with concepts that, in your native language, fit each description in the left-hand column. Write in your native language, if necessary, and then translate into English. In the right-hand column, write any concepts that you know of that, in English usage, fit each description at the left. Some concepts have been supplied to get you started.

	In My Native Language	In English
Things that have edges		a sheet of paper a city
Things that can be more noticeable by being out of the ordinary		a sheep an unusual style of clothing
Things that are not liquid but can "flow"		money a crowd of people

39

Things that are like impurities in a fluid		mentally unstable people in a group insects in the air

Chapter 2: Excluding, Not Being Part Of

Additional Vocabulary Quiz

I. Categorizing

Cross out the one item in each set that—*in its meaning as used in Chapter 2*—fit most poorly into the category. Be prepared to give reasons for your choice if your teacher asks you to.

Example:

Making schedules: ~~clock~~   calendar   appointment

Note: *Clock* is not totally unrelated to the category, but the other two terms relate more strongly.

Vocabulary related to:

1. **Getting bigger:**	contract	expand	spread
2. **Getting a job:**	short-list	applicant	tumor
3. **Things that grow:**	tumor	poll	culture
4. **Possible characteristics of a regulator:**	strict	illegible	punitive
5. **Unattractive people or things:**	an appealing idea	bland food	a misfit

II. Paraphrasing

Use the best item from the list to rephrase each statement. Change the form of the item if necessary to fit the grammar of the sentence. You may also change words in the sentence itself. Do not change the meaning of the original. Use each word from the list only once.

character	press
evidence	talented
overdue	

1. The strongest indication of Jackson's guilt was a set of fingerprints found at the crime scene.

   _____

   _____

2. Reporters and photographers kept following the Princess of Wales.

   _____

   _____

3. Heather showed a lot of natural internal strength by remaining calm while her roommates got upset.

   _____

   _____

4. The Corey Jones advertising company employs some people with a lot of natural ability in graphic design.

   _____

   _____

5. I sent an e-mail to Bart three weeks ago, and just today he sent me a response.

_____

_____

III. Applying the Vocabulary

The following list contains some methods used to control a disease called SARS (severe acute respiratory syndrome) in 2003. The most effective methods are at the top of the list, and the least effective are at the bottom. Using at least five additional vocabulary words from Chapter 2 (see page 217 of *BAV*), write an essay explaining why some of these methods probably were or were not effective. Your answer should deal with at least three of the methods, but you do not have to include all the methods on the list. Underline the words you use from Chapter 2.

Some Methods Used to Control SARS in 2003

Highly effective	Early identification of symptoms
↑	Campaigns to urge frequent and thorough hand-washing
	Quarantining proven victims separately from suspected victims
	Ensuring that conditions for quarantined persons were safe, clean, and non-threatening
	Closing schools, canceling sports events, etc.
	Issuing warnings about travel to affected areas
	Distributing breathing masks to bus passengers and others in crowded circumstances
	Disinfecting hotel rooms, restaurants, and other places known to have been visited by SARS victims
	Adopting laws to require those with symptoms to report to medical authorities
↓	Thermal scanning of domestic travelers to detect those with fevers
Not very effective	Thermal scanning of international air passengers to detect those with fevers

Chapter 2: Excluding, Not Being Part Of

Quiz 1

I. Fill in the Blanks

Fill in each blank with the best item from the list. Change the form of the item if necessary to fit the grammar of the sentence. Use each item from the list only once.

exclude	egregious
ban	marginal
rogue	filter

1. The department's economic statistics are misleading because they _____ such important things as the cost of health insurance.

2. The law in New Cambria _____ all political advertising two weeks before an election.

3. A _____ bison broke away from the herd and charged into downtown Deadwood.

4. Alison's _____ misbehavior in class has been distracting her classmates.

5. "Creek-bottom trees" such as cottonwoods can be large, but their wood is of only _____ value.

6. If teenagers in your house are accessing harmful Internet sites, you should ask your Internet service provider to _____ the content that can come to your house.

II. Paraphrasing

Use the best item from the list to rephrase each statement. Change the form of the item if necessary to fit the grammar of the sentence. You may also change words in the sentence itself. Do not change the meaning of the original statement. Use each item from the list only once.

alien	keep out
anomalous	outcast
exception	screen

1. The police academy carefully checks applicants to detect anyone who might have an unhealthy desire to use violence against suspects.

   _____

   _____

2. Ellie felt like she wasn't accepted by the other children in her neighborhood.

   _____

   _____

3. Almost every part of a raw potato is edible, but green patches on the skin are not.

   _____

   _____

4. The practice of calling one's parents by their first names seems strange to me.

    _____

    _____

5. Monotremes, which lay eggs instead of giving birth to live young, are not like other mammals.

    _____

    _____

III. Applying the Vocabulary

The chart that follows shows the limits imposed by the U.S. Constitution (including amendments) on who can become President of the United States. The right column, where possible, gives one or two examples of politicians who would be kept out of the presidential office by each requirement. Using at least five words from Chapter 2, summarize the information given in the chart. Your summary should be a full, well-connected paragraph. Underline the words you use from Chapter 2.

Note: This exercise requires no special knowledge. You can do it without knowing who any of the named politicians are. However, if you are interested, it is very easy to get basic information about these people over the Internet.

Who Can Become President of the United States?

Constitutional Requirement	Some Well-Known Politicians Affected
Must have been born in the United States or born abroad of parents who are U.S. citizens.	Arnold Schwarzenegger (born in Austria) Jennifer Granholm (born in Canada)
Must be at least 35 years old	U.S. Rep. Patrick McHenry of North Carolina (31 years old in 2006)
Must have lived in the United States for at least 14 years	Not an issue for currently well-known politicians
Must not have already been elected president twice	Bill Clinton (elected in 1992 and 1996)
President twice	George W. Bush (declared the winner in 2000 by the U.S. Supreme Court; elected in 2004)
Must not have served more than two years of another president's term AND must not have been elected to his or her own term	No living examples. Gerald Ford served more than two years of Richard Nixon's term in the 1970s, but Ford was never elected President on his own.

Chapter 2: Excluding, Not Being Part Of

Quiz 2

I. Sentence Completion

Circle the best item to complete each sentence. Be careful. In some items both choices might be possible, but one is a better choice than the other.

1. The survey showed that Bettina Sales was the most popular singer in the nation, but the researchers *(excluded/kept out)* people over the age of 25 from their sample.

2. Settlers from Europe took all the best farmland and left the native peoples with isolated patches of *(egregious/marginal)* land that produced little.

3. Before the hospital accepts a blood donation, it *(screens/filters)* for evidence of disease.

4. Crawford enjoyed portraying himself as an *(outcast/alien)*, misunderstood by a heartless society.

5. The religious leaders who ran the government *(banned/excluded)* all forms of public entertainment, such as movies, music, and plays.

II. Paraphrasing

Use the best item from the list to rephrase each statement. Change the form of the item if necessary to fit the grammar of the sentence. You may also change words in the sentence itself. Do not change the meaning of the original statement. Use each item from the list only once.

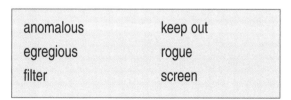

anomalous	keep out
egregious	rogue
filter	screen

1. Until Europeans began settling in Australia, its remote location prevented the animals of other continents from migrating there.

   _____

   _____

2. I usually drive faster than the speed limit, but I make sure my car blends into the traffic so the police don't notice me.

   _____

   _____

3. When the planet Venus appears to cross the sun (a transit of Venus), an unusual dark patch (called the black-drop effect) distorts the planet's outline near the edges of the sun.

   _____

   _____

4. One lone soldier broke away from his unit and started shooting, even though the commander had ordered all troops to stay where they were and not fire.

   _____

   _____

5. For not very much money, you can buy software that will examine your incoming e-mail and remove any spam (junk e-mail).

   _____

   _____

6. To control the company's public image, department managers insist that all news must flow through their offices before being released.

_____

_____

III. Applying the Vocabulary

Using at least five words from Chapter 2, summarize the information given. Your summary should be a full, well-connected paragraph. Underline the words you use from Chapter 2.

Types of Radiation Blocked by Material

Material	Alpha Particles	Beta Rays	Gamma Rays & X-Rays	Neutron Radiation
Paper	Yes	Only if at least 1/2 inch thick	No	No
Plastic	Yes for most types	Only if at least 1/2 inch thick	No	Yes by some types of plastic
Concrete	Yes	Yes	No	Yes
Water	A little bit	A little bit	No	Yes
Lead	Yes	Yes	Yes	No

Chapter 2: Excluding, Not Being Part Of

Quiz 3: Collocations and Common Phrases

I. Collocations and Common Phrases

Fill in each blank with the best item from the list. Not every item on the list will be used. Some items may be used more than once.

among	in that	social
between	inalienable rights	sole
elephant	of	state
from	out	through

1. Earth's atmosphere blocks most ultraviolet radiation, but some of it is still able to filter _____ to the surface.

2. South Dakota's Black Hills are anomalous _____ areas east of the 105th meridian _____ they contain several peaks higher than 7,000 feet.

3. I went to a boarding school where we had to wear a tie to every meal, the _____ exception being our last dinner of the year.

4. Higgins had easily detectable psychological problems, which caused him to be screened _____ of every job-application process.

5. When the writers of the Declaration of Independence said that all humans had certain _____, they meant that rights like life, liberty, and the pursuit of happiness should not be taken away.

6. Grandpa Crimmer was a grumpy old man, a _____ outcast who sat alone in his dark house and complained to himself about the world.

7. The president's assistants banned the reporter _____ the White House because they didn't like the newspaper articles she wrote.

8. The government of South Bentonia was very insulted that the U.S. labeled the country a rogue _____.

9. University officials struggled to keep a negative report _____ of the news.

II. Paraphrasing

Using the word in parentheses, rephrase each statement. Change the form of the item if necessary to fit the grammar of the sentence. You may also change words in the sentence itself. Do not change the meaning of the original item.

1. *(exclusive)* The governor's son tried to join the Alpha Tau fraternity, but they wouldn't let him in.

   _____

   _____

2. *(keep out)* Because citizens of Nejd-Nafar can easily buy satellite dishes and hide them, the government can't prevent outside ideas from coming into the kingdom.

   _____

   _____

3. *(outcast)* Jenna Peavey didn't really love Timmy Lee. She was just intrigued by the chance to change someone rejected by society into an acceptable person.

   _____

   _____

4. *(anomalous)* The electron telescopes on Mt. Taylor were picking up a strange radiation signal from a seemingly empty part of the galaxy.

_____

_____

5. *(ban)* The school board said that none of its members could talk about the meeting to anyone who wasn't there.

_____

_____

III. Applying the Vocabulary

Using at least five words from Chapter 2, summarize the reading passage "What Is, or Is Not, Europe?" (see the Appendix, pages 193–95). A beginning sentence for the summary has been written for you to help you get started. Use your own words. Underline the words you use from Chapter 2.

Summary

No matter what set of criteria is used, it is not easy to define the boundaries of the European continent.

Chapter 2: Excluding, Not Being Part Of

Quiz 4: Key Words and Related Word Forms

I. Fill in the Blanks

Fill in each blank with the best item from the list. Change the form of the item if necessary to fit the grammar of the sentence. Use each item only once.

anomaly	marginalize
cast out	screening
exclusive	

1. Grueneman moved to a different city because he felt like his group of friends had

   _____ him _____ for objecting to their heavy drinking.

2. A club that advertises itself as "_____" is probably not for me. I don't like

   people who take pride in keeping other people out.

3. The prime minister _____ several possible rivals by having the police plant

   drugs in their houses so they could be arrested and disgraced.

4. By sneaking dangerous weapons onto airplanes, reporters showed that airport

   _____ procedures were inadequate.

5. This year's rains in the southwest were an _____, producing in three months

   the amount of rain the region usually gets in three years.

II. Paraphrasing

Use the best item from the list to rephrase each statement. Change the form of the item if necessary to fit the grammar of the sentence. You may also change words in the sentence itself. Do not change the meaning of the original statement. Use each item from the list only once.

inalienable rights	excluding
sole exception	rogue state
egregious behavior	

1. The Borenalian prime minister accused Feringistan of being arrogant and uncontrollable, going its own way and causing a lot of trouble for other nations.

   _____

   _____

2. Liquirhine, a new decongestant, was approved for all patients except those who have had inner-ear problems.

   _____

   _____

3. The city decided to tear down old, uninhabited buildings, with the exception of historically protected structures and other culturally importnat buildings.

   _____

   _____

4. The U.S. Declaration of Independence spoke of certain rights that the government can't take away from people—life, liberty, and the pursuit of happiness.

_____

_____

5. The governor was embarrassed by her brother's unusual antics, such as his dancing on the tables at the inaugural ball.

_____

_____

III. Applying the Vocabulary

Using at least five words from Chapter 2, write a short biography of the Irish writer Oscar Wilde. You may use any facts from the list, but you do not have to use all of them. Your biography should be about 100–150 words long. Underline the words you use from Chapter 2.

Selected Events from the Life of Oscar Wilde (1854–1900)

- 1857—Wilde's ten-year-old sister, Isolda, dies of an unidentified disease. Oscar (now 13) is extremely shaken. For the rest of his life, he carries a lock of her hair in an envelope.

- 1872–1876—Wilde excels in academics at some of Ireland's best schools, including Trinity College in Dublin.

- 1886—Wilde's father dies. The family can no longer afford to let Wilde continue at university.

- 1881—Published his first volume of poems; went on a 240-day visit to America.

- 1884—Married Constance Lloyd. They had two sons in the next two years.

- 1890—Published the novel *The Picture of Dorian Gray* in an American magazine. Many Irish and English groups argue that it should not be published in their countries because they think it is indecent.

- 1892–1895—Published several hugely successful plays, including *Lady Windermere's Fan* and *The Importance of Being Earnest.*

- 1895—Wilde is accused by an aristocrat, the Marquis of Queensbury, of having a romantic relationship with the marquis's son, Boise. Wilde sues the marquis for libel. Wilde stops his lawsuit but is convicted of indecent conduct.

- 1895–1897—Wilde is jailed and forced to do hard labor.

- 1897—Wilde is released from jail. He writes *The Ballad of Reading Gaol* to describe the horrible conditions he endured.

- 1898—Wilde's wife, Constance, dies.

- 1898–1900—Wilde never re-enters the Irish or English literary mainstream. Produces no new works of any consequence.

- 1900—Dies of meningitis at the age of 46.

Unit 3

BLOCK 2
Similarities and Differences (*BAV* Chapters 3, 4, and 5)

Chapter 3: Equivalence, Similarity

Thinking about Metaphors

Fill in the middle column with concepts that, in your native language, fit each description in the left-hand column. Write in your native language, if necessary, and then translate into English. In the right-hand column, write any concepts that you know of that, in English usage, fit each description at the left. Some concepts have been supplied to get you started.

	In My Native Language	In English
Things that can achieve a certain level or standard		income a nation's military power

Things that can exist separately alongside each other, like lines that run in the same direction but never meet		two educational systems two people's experiences
Features that can make one person or thing seem like an exact copy of another		physical appearance style of writing
Things that can reach around other things, as if encircling them		borders of a country the limits of a group

Chapter 3: Equivalence, Similarity

Additional Vocabulary Quiz

I. Categorizing

Cross out the one item in each set that—*in its meaning as used in Chapter 3*—fits most poorly into the category. Be prepared to give reasons for your choice if your teacher asks you to.

Example:

Making schedules: ~~clock~~   calendar   appointment

Note: *Clock* is not totally unrelated to the category, but the other two terms relate more strongly.

Vocabulary related to:

1. **Living things:**	glacier	herb	robin
2. **Motion or lack of it:**	flow	defer to	stationary
3. **Size and strength:**	environmental	large-scale	understated
4. **Schools:**	admit	faculty	reggae
5. **Things made by people:**	design	natural resources	novel

II. Paraphrasing

Use the best item from the list to rephrase each statement. Change the form of the item, if necessary, to fit the grammar of the sentence. You may also change the words in the sentence itself. Do not change the meaning of the original statement. Use each word from the list only once.

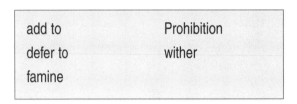

add to   Prohibition

defer to   wither

famine

1. Even though I don't agree with my lawyer's decisions, I think I have to step aside and trust her superior knowledge of how the courts work.

   _____

   _____

2. If you set up a computer network in your home, make sure you buy equipment that will allow you to connect more computers to it in the future.

   _____

   _____

3. During the holidays, no one watered the plants in the office so they dried up and died.

   _____

   _____

4. Several times in the late 20th century, lack of rain caused large parts of Africa to suffer severe and often deadly food shortages.

   _____

   _____

5. In the 1920s, the United States briefly made the production and consumption of alcoholic drinks illegal.

_____

_____

III. Applying the Vocabulary

The following is a list of some ways for an average individual or family to use less energy and help protect the natural environment. Using at least five additional vocabulary words from Chapter 3 (see page 217 of *BAV*), explain the benefits of some of these actions. Your answer should deal with at least three of these actions, but you should not try to mention all the actions on the list. Underline the words you use from Chapter 3.

- Use public transportation (buses, trains, etc.) instead of driving.
- Drive cars that get at least 30 miles per gallon on the highway.
- Seal the cracks around windows and doors during home-heating and home-cooling seasons.
- Clean filters in furnaces and air conditioners.
- Turn off lights and electrical appliances when not in use.
- Replace ordinary light bulbs with long-life bulbs.
- Use cloth instead of paper for napkins, diapers, cleaning cloths, etc.
- Recycle cans, bottles, newspaper, etc.
- Buy products made of recycled materials.

Chapter 3: Equivalence, Similarity

Quiz 1

I. Fill in the Blanks

Fill in each blank with the best item from the list. Change the form of the item if necessary to fit the grammar of the sentence. Use each item from the list only once.

alike	image
clone	just as
echo	parallel

1. While physicists in the United States were investigating the properties of nanocrystals, a _____ study was being carried out in Switzerland.

2. Insects and arachnids _____ derive their body shape from an exo-skeleton, not from an internal set of bones.

3. Jimmy Bergoni was dismissed by music critics as just another Italian-American crooner, a Sinatra _____, despite Bergoni's vocal inventiveness and his magnificent range.

4. _____ the Victorian British dominated world sea traffic, the U.S. had few rivals in the air or in space during the late 20th century.

5. A militant group calling itself the Khan's Army foolishly hoped to establish a new Mongol Empire in the _____ of the one ruled by Genghis Khan and his successors.

6. Contemporary teen slang unwittingly _____ the in-group speech of Southern California surfers during the late 1950s and early 1960s.

II. Paraphrasing

Use the best item from the list to rephrase each statement. Change the form of the item if necessary to fit the grammar of the sentence. You may also change words in the sentence itself. Do not change the meaning of the original statement. Use each item from the list only once

counterpart	likewise
equality	parity
identical	

1. A 40-year prison sentence for possessing small amounts of drugs is wrong. The severity of the punishment is not in line with the seriousness of the crime.

   _____

   _____

2. Because plants can pollinate themselves, the genetic make-up of an offspring can be exactly the same as that of its one parent.

   _____

   _____

3. The professional convention gave Jane a chance to meet many quality-control supervisors working for other companies.

   _____

   _____

4. The state of Vermont banned the importation of trash for burial in the state. The state of Minnesota imposed a similar ban.

_____

_____

5. If we want to ensure that all students have the same access to computer services, we have to set up labs throughout the campus.

_____

_____

III. Applying the Vocabulary

Using at least five words from Chapter 3, summarize the information given. Your summary should be a full, well-connected paragraph. Underline the words you use from Chapter 3.

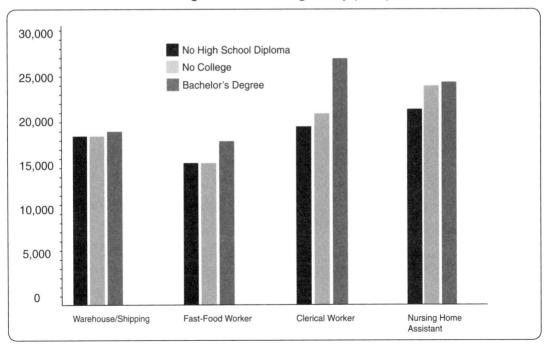

Average Annual Starting Salary (2004)

Note: Figures are for exercise purposes only. Not drawn from actual data.

Chapter 3: Equivalence, Similarity

Quiz 2

I. Sentence Completion

Circle the best item to complete each sentence. Be careful. In some sentences both choices might be possible, but one is a better choice than the other.

1. When there's no fruit on the plant, wild blackberries look almost *(identical/alike)* to wild raspberries.

2. When I flip through the Rubinski family album, I often remark that Helen is the very *(echo/image)* of her grandmother.

3. This shipment requires payment of $6,500 or the *(equality/equivalent)* in euros or Japanese yen.

4. The president of the United States is not an exact *(counterpart/parallel)* of the British prime minister, who can be swiftly removed from office by Parliament.

5. Some South Asian medical facilities are on a campaign to achieve *(equality/parity)* with North American and European hospitals in order to attract medical tourists—people who travel abroad for low-cost medical care.

II. Paraphrasing

Use the best item from the list to rephrase each statement. Change the form of the item if necessary to fit the grammar of the sentence. You may also change words in the sentence itself. Do not change the meaning of the original statement. Use each word from the list only once.

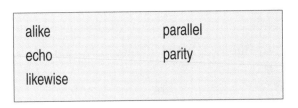

alike	parallel
echo	parity
likewise	

1. Recent steep increases in United States housing prices are strikingly similar to what happened in Japan during the early 1990s.

   _____

   _____

2. Both the teachers and the students denounced the new dress-code policy.

   _____

   _____

3. A U.S. university curriculum in nuclear physics followed a path similar to those at most European universities.

   _____

   _____

4. Verro Appliance Co. is trying to achieve the same market share as its competitors.

   _____

   _____

5. Joe is applying to medical schools, and Al is under pressure from his mom to do the same.

_____

_____

III. Applying the Vocabulary

Using at least five words from Chapter 3, summarize the information given. Your summary should be a full, well-connected paragraph. Underline the words you use from Chapter 3.

Properties of Two Common Components of Medicine for Colds and Coughs—Guaifenesin and Pseudoephedrine

	Guaifenesin	Pseudoephedrine
Similarity to natural compounds	Very similar to capsaicin, a natural component of hot peppers.	Somewhat similar in structure to epinephrine, a natural secretion of the adrenal gland.
Prime medicinal use	Expectorant. Breaks up thick mucus in respiratory tract; primarily prescribed for bronchitis or other persistent coughing.	Decongestant. Dries up the flow of mucus in the nasal tracts and sinuses.
Side effects	Rare. Dizziness or nausea may occur.	Moderately common, especially nervousness and sleeplessness. May become serious, leading to fear and anxiety.
Availability	In only a few over-the-counter multi-symptom cold medicines. Best known brand is Robitussin®.	In most over-the-counter multi-symptom cold medicines. Best known brand is Sudafed™. Availability is being restricted by law in many states.
Danger of addiction	Minimal	Slight, but can be used in the illegal manufacture of methamphetamines, which are addictive.
Cost	Low	Low, but likely to rise as governments restrict availability.

Chapter 3: Equivalence, Similarity

Quiz 3: Collocations and Common Phrases

I. Collocations and Common Phrases

Fill in each blank with the best item from the list. Not every item on the list will be used. Use each item only once.

achieve	her	qualifications
combination	in	the
division	in that	routes
essentially	of	virtually

1. Last year's break-up of Jezirastan into several ethnic territories echoed the _____ of the former Republic of Griana in the 1990s.

2. Secretary of Transportation Mary Rohler met with _____ Italian counterpart to discuss automotive technology.

3. The founders of the U.S. Central Intelligence Agency aimed to set up an external spying unit _____ the image of Britain's MI6.

4. The two senators responded to the reporter with _____ identical statements.

5. The trade corridor known as the Silk Road paralleled the invasion _____ used by Central Asian people to reach Europe.

6. In the 1600s, many nations tried to _____ full parity with the Dutch navy, but none did.

7. Alpha-amino acids are alike _____ their central sections contain one carboxylic-acid group (COOH) and one amino group (NH_2).

8. The job requires a master's degree and three years' experience, or an equivalent _____.

II. Paraphrasing

Using the word in parentheses, rephrase each statement. Change the form of the item if necessary to fit the grammar of the sentence. You may also change words in the sentence itself. Do not change the meaning of the original statement.

1. *(equality)* Members of Congress have a responsibility to respect the American consensus that all citizens should be treated the same.

    _____

    _____

2. *(likewise)* The planets Mercury, Venus, and Mars sometimes exhibit retrograde motion, an apparent backward course across the night sky.

    _____

    _____

3. *(clone)* People hoping to be distinctive in their fashionable clothing often end up looking just like one another.

    _____

    _____

4. *(just as)* Students were shocked by the principal's decision to cancel all field trips. So were the teachers.

_____

_____

5. (alike) Both the Korean and Japanese languages have some syllable-based sets of characters in their writing systems.

_____

_____

III. Applying the Vocabulary

Using at least five words from Chapter 3, summarize the reading passage "Generic Pharmaceuticals" (see the Appendix, pages 196–97). A beginning sentence for the summary has been written, to help you get started. Use your own words. Underline the words you use from Chapter 3.

Summary

Under some conditions, consumers can pay less for medicines by buying generic drugs instead of well-known brand-name drugs.

Chapter 3: Equivalence, Similarity

Quiz 4: Key Words and Related Word Forms

I. Fill in the Blanks

Fill in each blank with the best item from the list. Change the form of the item if necessary to fit the grammar of the sentence. Use each item from the list only once.

cloning	identity
echo	like
equivalence	parallel

1. The panda looks so much _____ a bear that most zoo visitors believe it is one.

2. The success of our basketball team this year sounded an _____ of our last championship season more than 30 years ago.

3. Before Grantsburg College can give you credit for courses taken at another college, the registrar has to have evidence of _____ between those courses and Grantsburg's.

4. A tight security system establishes the _____ of every visitor by means of fingerprints, iris scans, or the measurement of some other physical characteristic.

5. There are many _____ between the climate recently and that of a time called the Medieval Warm Period.

6. _____ produces an organism genetically identical to the "parent."

II. Paraphrasing

Use the best item from the list to rephrase each statement. Change the form of the item if necessary to fit the grammar of the sentence. You may also change words in the sentence itself. Do not change the meaning of the original statement. Use each item from the list only once.

counterpart	image
equally	parallel
equivalent	

1. Through the Sister Cities program, our mayor got to meet the mayor of Sendai, Japan.

   _____

   _____

2. One candidate for the job was just as qualified as the other.

   _____

   _____

3. The average worker in Costa Brava earns a wage of 180 bravitos per week, which is the same as about US$30.

   _____

   _____

4. In her wedding dress, Marlene looks exactly like her grandmother looks in old wedding pictures.

   _____

   _____

5. Even though Alec studied in England and Harvey went to the University of Arizona, their doctoral coursework followed similar paths.

   _____

   _____

III. Applying the Vocabulary

The table outlines two experiments. Using at least five words from Chapter 3, summarize the information. Your answer should be a full, well-connected paragraph about 100 words long. Underline the words you use from Chapter 3.

A Comparison of Two Experiments

	Prof. Tawfiq's Experiments	Prof. Malone's Experiments
Researcher's position	Chair, Department of Public Health	Chair, Department of Public Health
Location	University of Cairo (Egypt)	University of Idaho (USA)
Time	1999–present	1999–present
Research question	How does the oxygen level of an environment affect the reproduction of the bacterium *E. coli*?	How does the oxygen level of an environment affect the reproduction of the bacterium *E. coli*?
Experimental subjects	500 healthy humans	350 healthy humans
Funding	Egyptian pounds 3,618,750	US$625,000 Note: 100 US dollars = 579 Egyptian pounds
Number of research assistants	15	16
Tentative results	There is no evidence of any significant effect of oxygen level on the reproduction of *E. coli*.	No evidence has yet been found to indicate that oxygen levels affect the reproduction of *E. coli*.

Chapter 4: Difference, Inequality

Thinking about Metaphors

Fill in the middle column with concepts that, in your native language, fit each description in the left-hand column. Write in your native language, if necessary, and then translate into English. In the right-hand column, write any concepts that you know of that, in English usage, fit each description at the left. Some concepts have been supplied to get you started.

	In My Native Language	In English
Things that can follow the same path for some distance and then follow different directions, like branches of a river		opinions two persons' careers
Things that can have a somewhat unpleasant empty space between them, like two separated front teeth		two political positions the expected and actual achievements of a student
Things that can be prepared or formed in different ways, like rice or meat or some other food		two persons' careers two nations' policies

Things that may or may not harmonize, like two sounds		the expected quality of a movie and its actual quality what someone says and what is true

Chapter 4: Difference, Inequality

Additional Vocabulary Quiz

I. Categorizing

Cross out the one item in each set that—*in its meaning as used in Chapter 4*—fits most poorly into the category. Be prepared to give reasons for your choice if your teacher asks you to.

> **Example:**
>
> Making schedules: ~~clock~~   calendar   appointment
>
> Note: *Clock* is not totally unrelated to the category, but the other two terms relate more strongly.

Vocabulary related to:

1. **Money that you make:**   income   infrastructure   revenue
2. **Serious social disruptions:**   auditor   revolution   tornado
3. **Confusion or uncertainty:**   disturbing   massive   puzzling
4. **Positive personality traits:** immoral   innocent   savvy
5. **Ensuring proper business practices:**   auditor   portfolio   regulation

II. Paraphrasing

Use the best item from the list to rephrase each statement. Change the form of the item if necessary to fit the grammar of the sentence. You may also change words in the sentence itself. Do not change the meaning of the original statement. Use each word from the list only once.

attend to	otherwise
boom	respond
career	

1. Adequate security in school buildings involves not just protection from threats but also effective response to an emergency once it has started.

   _____

   _____

2. I just don't have time to do something about every problem expressed by members of our staff.

   _____

   _____

3. Many musicians can learn the guitar well enough to have some fun with it, but very few are able to actually make a living as a professional guitarist.

   _____

   _____

4. Investors who plan for the long term are not impressed by the sudden popularity and price rises of things like real estate or Internet-related stocks.

   _____

   _____

5. It's a good idea to dig a shallow trench around the base of your tent so that if heavy rain falls, it won't flow under your tent.

_____

_____

III. Applying the Vocabulary

Using at least five additional vocabulary words from Chapter 4 (see pages 217–18 of *BAV*), summarize the information given. Your summary should be a full, well-connected paragraph. Underline the words you use from Chapter 4.

Likelihood of Success for Small Businesses
(5 = very high; 1 = very low)

Type of Small Business	Likelihood of Success after 1 Year	Likelihood of Success after 5 Years
Apartment management	5	5
Day-care for children	4	4
Doctor's office	5	5
Grocery store	3	1
Home construction	3	1
Investment counselor	3	1
Law office	5	1
Plumbing	4	1
Religion-oriented business (sales of religious articles, etc.)	5	5
Restaurant & deli	4	1
Trucking	2	1
Vegetable farming	5	5

Chapter 4: Difference, Inequality

Quiz 1

I. Fill in the Blanks

Fill in each blank with the best item from the list. Change the form of the item if necessary to fit the grammar of the sentence. Use each item from the list only once.

contrast	disparate
differentiate	disparity
discrete	inequality

1. The great _____ in wealth between rich and poor countries cannot be entirely blamed on differences in climate.

2. The cultural history of humans broadly embraces the _____ histories of particular groups.

3. Van Leeuwenhoek's microscope offered a captivating view of _____ cells, each with its own fence-like wall, inside a seemingly indivisible piece of cork.

4. Social _____ usually leads to what we will call medical stratification, the separation of a society into classes determined by such health factors as obesity, rates of HIV infection, and the incidence of certain cancers.

5. The team's stunning success in the tournament _____ markedly with their winless record in the regular season.

6. When children work with crayons (or colored pencils) to fill in outlined figures, their ability to _____ among colors improves.

II. Paraphrasing

Use the best item from the list to rephrase each statement. Change the form of the item if necessary to fit the grammar of the sentence. You may also change words in the sentence itself. Do not change the meaning of the original statement. Use each word from the list only once.

differ	diverge
discrepancy	diverse
distinguish	heterogeneous

1. People from many different countries live in America.

   _____

   _____

2. One word may have many meanings. Only by looking at the context can one choose the intended meaning among all others.

   _____

   _____

3. Students of English as a Foreign Language may plan to use their English for many purposes.

   _____

   _____

4. Senators Burton and Craft expressed similar views about environmental law until the last election campaign.

   _____

   _____

5. Her performance on the final test did not fit in with the rest of her grades from the semester.

_____

_____

III. Applying the Vocabulary

Using at least five words from Chapter 4, summarize the information given. Your summary should be a full, well-connected paragraph. Underline the words you use from Chapter 4.

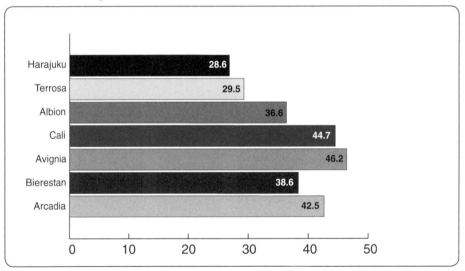

Percentage of Income Paid in Taxes, Selected Countries, 2006

Country	Percentage
Harajuku	28.6
Terrosa	29.5
Albion	36.6
Cali	44.7
Avignia	46.2
Bierestan	38.6
Arcadia	42.5

Note: Figures are for exercise purposes only. Not drawn from actual data.

Chapter 4: Difference, Inequality

Quiz 2

I. Sentence Completion

Circle the best item to complete each sentence. Be careful. In some sentences both choices might be possible, but one is a better choice than the other.

1. The country's *(diverse/heterogeneous)* and constantly growing economy has helped many business owners succeed.

2. Parents can somehow see each twin or triplet or even quadruplet as a *(discrete/disparate)* person, even if other people cannot tell one child from another.

3. The newspaper article focused on the *(contrast/inequality)* between the two candidates' reputations—Venema for his brilliant intellect, Boscomi for his astounding lack of knowledge about the world.

4. The complexity of relations between dominant and disadvantaged groups in the United States results from the nation's remarkably *(heterogeneous/discrete)* population.

5. Polls *(differ/diverge)* on how many people actually speak more than one language. Some polls show more than 50 percent, while others show just under 35 percent.

II. Paraphrasing

Use the best item from the list to rephrase each statement. Change the form of the item if necessary to fit the grammar of the sentence. You may also change words in the sentence itself. Do not change the meaning of the original statement. Use each item from the list only once.

differ	distinguish
differentiate	diverge
disparity	inequality

1. In many countries, women have almost the same job opportunities as men have.

   _____

   _____

2. John believes that his university degree, a Master's in Business Administration, will help him stand out from other job applicants.

   _____

   _____

3. Great imbalances in wealth could lead to political instability in newly prosperous countries.

   _____

   _____

4. The university president initially agreed with most professors about the mission of the university, but her views and theirs are now miles apart.

   _____

   _____

5. The two families share religious beliefs, but they do not agree on what their children should be allowed to do.

   _____

   _____

6. A line of animal stem cells comprises several generations of versatile cells that have not yet begun to take on the characteristics of a brain cell, a liver cell, or any other particular bodily component.

   _____

   _____

III. Applying the Vocabulary

Using at least five words from Chapter 4, summarize the information given. Your summary should be a full, well-connected paragraph. Underline the words you use from Chapter 4.

African Americans in New York and North Carolina, 1860

	New York	North Carolina
Slave population	0	331,000
Free black population	49,000	30,400
Free blacks allowed to vote?	Yes, but only men who owned property.	No. Voting rights for free black men were taken away in 1835.
Free blacks allowed to own property?	Yes	Yes
Number of free black U.S. citizens*	0	0
Estimated literacy rate among all blacks**	About 35%	About 5%

*The U.S. Supreme Court ruled in 1857 *(Dred Scott v. Sanford)* that blacks, whether free or slave, did not have U.S. citizenship.
**Exact figures not available.

Chapter 4: Difference, Inequality

Quiz 3: Collocations and Common Phrases

I. Collocations and Common Phrases

Fill in each blank with the best item from the list. Not every item on the list will be used. Some items may be used more than once.

between	intervals	significant
candidates	investments	stark
drops	parts	
from	population	

1. The two courses were discrete _____ one another, despite being taught by the same instructor.

2. It is difficult to distinguish _____ identical twins.

3. John decided to diversify his _____ for a safer return.

4. The _____ disparity among races in the rise of AIDS cases is the focus of a new report released today.

5. In the United States, ESL students form a very heterogeneous _____.

6. Because a large, complicated piece of furniture has disparate _____, it can be difficult for someone to put together without detailed instructions.

7. Ms. Booth liked her days to progress smoothly, not to separate unpredictably into discrete _____ of activity.

8. The two students' study habits were in _____ contrast to one another.

9. Several important attributes that differentiate job _____ should be considered when hiring an applicant.

10. As I splashed, the drops of water seemed to hang in the air long enough to be experienced as discrete _____ and had a beauty I couldn't describe.

II. Paraphrasing

Using the word in parentheses, rephrase each statement. Change the form of the item if necessary to fit the grammar of the sentence. You may also change words in the sentence itself. Do not change the meaning of the original statement.

1. *(inequality)* The time has come for us to fight against the unfair treatment of people, whether because of race, gender, or social class.

   _____

   _____

2. *(differ)* Even though her ideas are not similar to the committee's recommendations, they are still quite good and should be considered.

   _____

   _____

3. *(diverge)* One sociologist found that after ten years of marriage, women's views are no longer similar to those of their husbands.

   _____

   _____

4. *(distinguish)* What makes the sluggishness in the economy now unlike that of ten years ago is debt.

   _____

   _____

5. *(disparity)* A reporter on National Public Radio claimed that women did more work than men but they were paid less money.

   _____

   _____

III. Applying the Vocabulary

Using at least five words from Chapter 4, summarize the reading passage "Unequal Distribution of Wealth (see the Appendix, pages 198–99). A beginning sentence for the summary has been written for you to help you get started. Your summary should be a well-connected paragraph of 100 to 150 words. Use your own words. Underline the words you use from Chapter 4.

Summary

Differences in income between the wealthiest Americans and everyone else have increased dramatically during recent years.

Chapter 4: Difference, Inequality

Quiz 4: Key Words and Related Word Forms

I. Fill in the Blanks

Fill in each blank with the best item from the list. Change the form of the item if necessary to fit the grammar of the sentence. Use each item only once.

contrast	diverge
discrete	diverse
distinguish	

1. The new concert series will be very interesting. The composer-musicians come from

   _____ backgrounds ranging from classical to rock and roll.

2. Mark's amiability presents a pleasant _____ to his cousin Susie's snobbish

   aggressiveness.

3. In their earliest years, children cannot easily _____ between truth and lies.

4. Because the two friends will not see each other for years, their interests may

   _____.

5. A variety of small, _____ tasks is often easier to accomplish than one major

   goal.

II. Paraphrasing

Use the best item from the list to rephrase each statement. Change the form of the item if necessary to fit the grammar of the sentence. You may also change words in the sentence itself. Do not change the meaning of the original statement. Use each word from the list only once.

differ	disparity
differentiate	inequality
disparate	

1. The committee could not reach an agreement. Susan believed the event should be free, Jeff believed tickets should cost a small amount, and Jill believed ticket prices should be higher.

   _____

   _____

2. Phil micro-manages his business, concerning himself with every small detail, while Chris takes a broader macro-management approach.

   _____

   _____

3. An infant separated from his or her mother can suffer a severe emotional shock, since the infant does not truly recognize that the mother is a separate person.

   _____

   _____

4. Some people fly their flags at half-mast only when a public servant or soldier dies, whereas others do so when any notable person passes away.

   _____

   _____

5. In some countries, women do not yet hold the right to vote, while their husbands and sons have been voting for decades.

_____

_____

III. Applying the Vocabulary

Using at least five words from Chapter 4, answer the question that follows. Your answer should be a full, well-connected paragraph of about 100 words. Underline the words you use from Chapter 4.

This chart details economic and social conditions in Gahwah and Halib, two regions of the Republic of Alfirdos, at two points in history. In your opinion, what are the most important differences between the two regions?

A Comparison of Economic and Social Conditions in Two Countries

	Gahwah		Halib	
	1990	Present	1990	Present
Per capita annual income (converted to present-day U.S. dollars)	$4,309	$11,268	$4,700	$28,068
Unemployment rate	24%	15%	21%	5%
Literacy rate for men	56%	87%	63%	98%
Literacy rate for women	13%	21%	13%	22%
Average lifespan for men	48 years	53 years	43 years	73 years
Average lifespan for women	67 years	67 years	67 years	77 years
Birthrate (per 10,000 people)	143	217	128	78
Population	478,069	1.73 million	506,078	660, 000

Chapter 5: Changes, Increases, Decreases

Thinking about Metaphors

Fill in the middle column with concepts that, in your native language, fit each description in the left-hand column. Write in your native language, if necessary, and then translate into English. In the right-hand column, write any concepts that you know of that, in English usage, fit each description at the left. Some concepts have been supplied to get you started.

	In My Native Language	In English
Things that can go across from one condition to another		someone's attitude toward something a nation's economy
Things that can have a structure, like a house or some other building		a company's production system a religion
Things that can have speed		time economic processes, such as rises in price

Things that can go downhill		someone's health
		someone's abilities,
		  such as the ability
		  to remember names

Chapter 5: Changes, Increases, Decreases

Additional Vocabulary Quiz

I. Categorizing

Cross out the one item in each set that—*in its meaning as used in Chapter 5*—fits most poorly into the category. Be prepared to give reasons for your choice if your teacher asks you to.

Example:

Making schedules: ~~clock~~ calendar appointment

Note: *Clock* is not totally unrelated to the category, but the other two terms relate more strongly.

Vocabulary related to:

1. **Human biology:**	consensus	eyesight	genome
2. **Money:**	debt	financial	militant
3. **Control by someone else:**	dependence	dominated	veteran
4. **Things found in nature:**	atmosphere	fossil fuels	scandal
5. **A container of liquid:**	fuel-efficient	leak	seal

II. Paraphrasing

Use the best item from the list to rephrase each statement. Change the form of the item if necessary to fit the grammar of the sentence. You may also change words in the sentence itself. Do not change the meaning of the original statement. Use each item from the list only once.

consensus	run on
fatigue	scandal
financial	

1. Along with a high fever, Carl had severe muscle aches and felt deeply tired.

   _____

   _____

2. Ms. Terrell had to resign from her job because the public became outraged about her improper hiring practices.

   _____

   _____

3. Cars with diesel engines generally get better mileage than gasoline-powered cars.

   _____

   _____

4. Most people in our state agree that mature forests should not be cut down to make way for development.

   _____

   _____

5. The renovation of the stadium had to be postponed because there was not enough money to continue with it.

_____

_____

III. Applying the Vocabulary

Using at least five additional vocabulary words from Chapter 5 (see page 218 of *BAV*), summarize the information given. Your summary should be a full, well-connected paragraph. Underline the words you use from Chapter 5.

Fact Sheet: The Hanford Nuclear Reservation

Location	Eastern Washington State, North and West of Richland
Size	560 square miles
Bodies of water	the Columbia River
Characterization	Hanford is the largest nuclear waste dump in the Americas.
History	From World War II to the late 1980s, nuclear reactors at Hanford produced plutonium for use in nuclear weapons. The process involved passing water from the river through the reactors and then returning contaminated water to the river. Other wastes were put into 177 large underground tanks. Hanford stopped producing plutonium in 1987.
Current situation	At least 70 tanks have corroded, releasing highly poisonous liquid waste into the groundwater, which eventually reaches the Columbia River.
Attempts to fix the problem	Department of Energy teams pump remaining waste from corroded tanks to other tanks. Cement might be used to solidify other waste to keep it from flowing. No practical plan has yet been adopted to stop already released waste from reaching the Columbia River.

Source: U.S. Department of Energy, "The Hanford Site." Accessed March 25, 2006, *www.hanford.gov.*

Chapter 5: Changes, Increases, Decreases

Quiz 1

I. Fill in the Blanks

Fill in each blank with the best item from the list. Change the form of the item if necessary to fit the grammar of the sentence. Use each item from the list only once.

accelerate	expand
contract	modify
decline	transform

1. While there have been efforts to _____ the health-care system to serve a wider range of people, little has actually been accomplished.

2. The drama program's funding _____ to the point where it could no longer present two plays each year.

3. To please the majority of stockholders, the board of directors will have to slightly _____ its restructuring proposal.

4. The last leaders of the Soviet Union took several steps to modernize the economy and _____ the growth of private enterprise.

5. In the not too distant future, technology will _____ the way the news is delivered to individuals.

6. Some headaches result from rapid changes in the size of blood vessels, which first _____, then overdilate.

II. Paraphrasing

Use the best item from the list to rephrase each statement. Change the form of the items if necessary to fit the grammar of the sentence. You may also change words in the sentence itself. Do not change the meaning of the original statement. Use each item from the list only once.

diminish	reduce
raise	transform
redesign	

1. The Ridgeline Association hoped to make the local deforestation problem known to more people.

   _____

   _____

2. Working in the refugee camps caused Beth to become a different person.

   _____

   _____

3. The Internet has made the amount of time we wait to correspond with someone shorter.

   _____

   _____

4. The magazine wants to expand its audience, so it has plans to change the layout, as well as its features and ads.

   _____

   _____

5. In the years following the Cold War, the army of the Soviet Union gradually got smaller.

_____

_____

III. Applying the Vocabulary

Using at least five words from Chapter 5, summarize the information given. Your summary should be a full, well-connected paragraph. Underline the words you use from Chapter 5.

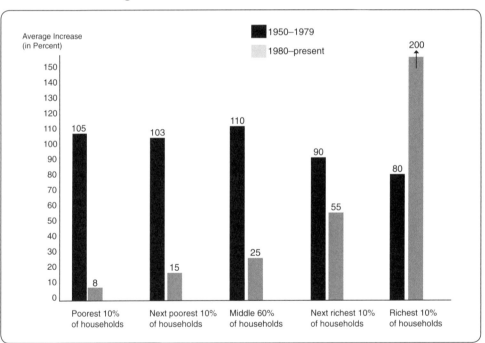

Average Increases in Household After-Tax Income

Note: Figures are for exercise purposes only. Not drawn from actual data.

Chapter 5: Changes, Increases, Decreases

Quiz 2

I. Sentence Completion

Circle the best item to complete each sentence. Be careful. In some sentences both choices might be possible, but one is a better choice than the other.

1. The state legislature is considering a plan to *(alter/restructure)* the entire system of state-funded colleges and universities.

2. The level of unemployment is likely to *(rise/accelerate)* as more factories close.

3. Putting the military under civilian control is an important step in the country's *(alteration/transition)* to democratic government.

4. To meet the demand for his new invention, Zach's production facilities had to *(transform/expand)* beyond the little machine shop in his garage.

5. Sugar can *(diminish/contract)* the function of the immune system, leaving a person more susceptible to illness.

II. Paraphrasing

Use the best item from the list to rephrase each statement. Change the form of the item if necessary to fit the grammar of the sentence. You may also change words in the sentence itself. Do not change the meaning of the original statement. Use each item from the list only once.

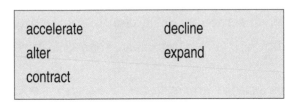

accelerate	decline
alter	expand
contract	

1. Some senators made changes to the proposed law so it could more easily be approved by the Senate as a whole.

   _____

   _____

2. In order for the company to increase its business, it must search for more new clients.

   _____

   _____

3. As gas prices went lower and lower, more people began to buy bigger cars and travel more on the highways.

   _____

   _____

4. The two governments hope to hasten the progress of peace in the region.

   _____

   _____

5. Einstein's laws of relativity proposed that under the right conditions time can dilate and space can become smaller.

_____

_____

III. Applying the Vocabulary

Using at least five words from Chapter 5, summarize the information given. Your summary should be a full, well-connected paragraph. Underline the words you use from Chapter 5.

Domestic Motor Vehicle Sales (in thousands)

Type of Vehicle	2004	2000	1996	1995	1992	1990	1988	1985	1980
Passenger Cars									
Domestics	7, 017	7,955	7,254	7,129	6,277	6,897	7,526	8,205	6,581
Imports	4,224	2,071	1,273	1,506	1,938	2,403	3,004	2,838	2,398
Light Trucks									
Utility	355	252	243	144	51	68	90	108	108
Van	338	314	254	274	241	254	302	261	172
Pick-up	954	900	936	967	524	568	666	628	546
Station wagon (on a truck chassis)	106	82	137	109	80	85	104	95	39
Sport Utility Vehicles (SUVs)	208	244	212	170	83	24	NA*	NA	NA

Source: Adapted from U.S. Dept. of Commerce data for 1980 to 1996. Figures for later years and all figures for SUVs are fictional and for exercise purposes only.

*NA = Figures not available.

Chapter 5: Changes, Increases, Decreases

Quiz 3: Collocations and Common Phrases

I. Collocations and Common Phrases

Fill in each blank with the best item from the list. Not every item on the list will be used. Some items may be used more than once.

behavior	development	influence
by	equally	into
chemicals	from	of
conflict	heart disease	plants
course	in	treatment

1. Healthier eating and regular exercise transformed Albert _____ a dangerously obese teenager _____ a healthy, fit young man.

2. Accelerating the _____ of children's basic reading skills is the main aim of Buffy's Language School.

3. Some _____ raise the level of nitrogen in the soil where they grow.

4. Early psychological experiments showed that a technique called operant conditioning could be used to modify a subject's _____.

5. Ironically, a sharp rise _____ biological activity may precede the collapse of the ecosystem in a lake or pond.

6. A patient's attitude can alter the _____ of a disease, with the most optimistic patients likely to see shorter, less severe bouts of illness.

7. In a flexible container, water expands _____ in all directions as it freezes.

8. During childbirth, the contraction _____ muscles in the uterus pushes the baby into the birth canal.

9. Immediate _____ can reduce the damage done by a heart attack.

10. The overuse of military power diminishes a nation's overall international

   _____.

II. Paraphrasing

Using the word in parentheses, rephrase each statement. Change the form of the item if necessary to fit the grammar of the sentence. You may also change words in the sentence itself. Do not change the meaning of the original statement.

1. *(transition)* The couple is experiencing a period of change as their children go to college and they move to a new city.

   _____

   _____

2. *(redesign)* Teacher-training institutes must revise their credential programs to include professional development credits.

   _____

   _____

3. *(restructure)* New regulations have forced the company to change the entire set of principles on which its benefits plan was built.

   _____

   _____

4. *(restrict)* Many senators support new legislation that will limit immigration.

_____

_____

5. *(contract)* During a heartbeat, the ventricles become smaller, pushing blood out of the heart into large blood vessels.

_____

_____

III. Applying the Vocabulary

Using at least five words from Chapter 5, summarize the reading passage "Extreme Weather" (see the Appendix, pages 200–1). A beginning sentence for the summary has been written for you to help you get started. Your summary should be a well-connected paragraph of 100 to 150 words. Use your own words. Underline the words you use from Chapter 5.

Summary

Some skeptics say that Earth's weather only seems to be getting more extreme, that in reality we are better at measuring weather phenomena so we simply notice the extremes that have been there all along.

Chapter 5: Changes, Increases, Decreases

Quiz 4: Key Words and Related Word Forms

I. Fill in the Blanks

Fill in each blank with the best item from the list. Change the form of the item if necessary to fit the grammar of the sentence. Use each item only once.

alter	rise
expand	transform
raise	

1. A dry summer and a poor crop of wild berries forced the bears to _____ their foraging range.

2. In a TV show called *Save My Car*, experts _____ an ordinary person's used car into a luxurious, high-tech marvel.

3. Tough talk by the U.S. president _____ the level of concern about a U.S. attack on the desert kingdom of Wadi Khali.

4. If you want to drive this car in high mountains, you should _____ the engine to function well in thinner air.

5. As a country's per capita income _____, its birthrate usually falls.

II. Paraphrasing

Use the best item from the list to rephrase each statement. Change the form of the item if necessary to fit the grammar of the sentence. You may also change words in the sentence itself. Do not change the meaning of the original statement. Use each word from the list only once.

contract	reduce
decline	restructure
modify	

1. In extreme heat or cold, the spider's egg sack shrinks to only about one-half its normal size.

   _____

   _____

2. Many students take evening English-pronunciation classes that concentrate on minimizing their accents.

   _____

   _____

3. As book printing became more reliant on electronic equipment, printers and publishers had to invent totally new ways of organizing their production departments.

   _____

   _____

4. You should make a few slight changes in your presentation to Mr. DeFord, who is well known for letting religion influence his business decisions.

   _____

   _____

5. Through the middle to late 1990s, the number of hurricanes striking Florida became dramatically lower.

_____

_____

III. Applying the Vocabulary

Using at least five words from Chapter 5, answer the question. Your answer should be a full, well-connected paragraph of about 100 words. Underline the words you use from Chapter 5.

- -

Typically, an economy develops in several stages. The first stage often involves the extraction of natural resources, such as minerals, timber, or petroleum. The economy may then move toward pollution-intensive manufacturing—steelmaking, chemical manufacture, etc. After a period in which manufacturing moves toward lighter, less-damaging pursuits such as the production of electronic components, the economy may progress to providing mainly services (accountancy, engineering, etc.) or information (data processing, movies or music for export, computer-aided design, and so forth).

- -

In your opinion, why is this pattern so common among economies? You do not have to be an expert to answer this question. An answer based on your personal observations and on simple reasoning is good enough.

Unit 4

Correlation, Causation, and Facilitation (*BAV* Chapters 6, 7, 8, and 9)

Chapter 6: Links, Correlations, Happening Together

Thinking about Metaphors

Fill in the middle column with concepts that, in your native language, fit each description in the left-hand column. Write in your native language, if necessary, and then translate into English. In the right-hand column, write any concepts that you know of that, in English usage, fit each description at the left. Some concepts have been supplied to get you started.

	In My Native Language	In English
Things that can be closely connected to each other, like links in a chain		a nation's wealth and its power a disease and an environmental problem

113

Things that travel closely with other things, like one friend with another		the symptoms of a disease (with the disease itself) happiness (with a job you like)
Things that can be measured in incremental degrees, like temperature		emotions success
Traits that can be carved deeply into something else, like letters made by cutting into stone		a certain accent a way of building houses that is typical in a certain nation

Chapter 6: Links, Correlations, Happening Together

Additional Vocabulary Quiz

I. Categorizing

Cross out the one item in each set that—*in its meaning as used in Chapter 6*— fits most poorly into the category. Be prepared to give reasons for your choice if your teacher asks you to.

Example:

Making schedules: ~~clock~~ calendar appointment

<u>Note</u>: *Clock* is not totally unrelated to the category, but the other two terms relate more strongly.

Vocabulary related to:

1. **Signs of sickness or injury:**	ache	algae	fever
2. **Vegetation:**	algae	freckle	millet
3. **Things operated by hand:**	cello	lactase	pliers
4. **Possible results of mental illness:**	baldness	depression	suicide
5. **Factors affecting the size of a population:**	birthrate	immigration	wage

II. Paraphrasing

Use the best item from the list to rephrase each statement. Change the form of the item if necessary to fit the grammar of the sentence. You may also change words in the sentence itself. Do not change the meaning of the original statement. Use each item from the list only once.

adulthood	emphasize
affluent	time zone
chain	

1. The time is officially the same everywhere in China, from Urumqi in the far west to Shanghai on the east coast.

   _____

   _____

2. Many movies directed by John Hughes are set in the wealthy suburbs north and northwest of Chicago.

   _____

   _____

3. To pull a car out of a ditch, you need a big truck and something stronger than a rope to link the car to the truck.

   _____

   _____

4. The spread of vine-borers can only be stopped by killing the insects before they mature.

   _____

   _____

5. The dean made a special point of telling us that attendance at the meeting was not optional.

   _____

   _____

III. Applying the Vocabulary

Using at least five additional vocabulary words from Chapter 6 (see page 218 of *BAV*), explain the information given. Your summary should be a full, well-connected paragraph. Underline the words you use from Chapter 6.

- -

A political action committee took a survey of 500 residents of the town of Forbes Creek. The survey asked respondents to indicate which of several possible threats they were most worried about. The chart that follows shows the percentages of respondents who rated each threat as their most serious concern.

- -

Major Concerns among Residents of Forbes Creek

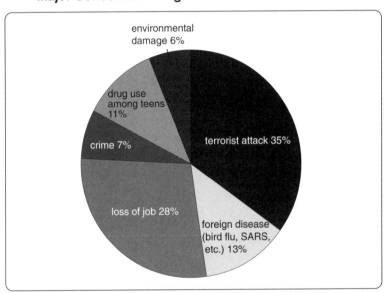

Note: Figures are for exercise purposes only. Not drawn from actual data.

Chapter 6: Links, Correlations, Happening Together

Quiz 1

I. Fill in the Blanks

Fill in each blank with the best item from the list. Change the form of the item if necessary to fit the grammar of the sentence. Use each item from the list only once.

accompany	imply
characteristic of	infer
correlation	go along with

1. Low river levels at Yellowstone Park in May _____ a lack of snowfall in the mountains during the previous winter.

2. Pictures often _____ the text in books meant for young readers.

3. We can _____ Viking ancestry from Mr. Ryan's red hair and freckles.

4. A gender system for nouns, in which some are masculine and others feminine, is _____ Romance languages such as Spanish, French, and Italian.

5. Responsibility for your own behavior _____ growing up and becoming independent of your parents.

6. In a reliable test, there is a strong _____ between the results of the test and the test-takers' actual skill or knowledge.

II. Paraphrasing

Use the best item from the list to rephrase each statement. Change the form of the item if necessary to fit the grammar of the sentence. You may also change words in the sentence itself. Do not change the meaning of the original statement. Use each item from the list only once.

associated with	link
characteristic of	to the degree that
in conjunction with	

1. One feature of Prairie Style architecture is the combination of rough natural materials, such as fieldstone, with smooth, clear-finished wood and broad expanses of glass.

   _____

   _____

2. Numerous surveys have shown that, all other factors being roughly equal, workers with at least one college degree earn about twice as much as do workers with only a high school diploma.

   _____

   _____

3. Scientists have long known there is a connection between obesity and diabetes.

   _____

   _____

4. Advertising is more effective if ads in print media are run at the same time as are television commercials with a similar approach.

   _____

   _____

5. The higher a nation's per capita income, the more divorce its families experience.

_____

_____

III. Applying the Vocabulary

Using at least five additional vocabulary words from Chapter 6, summarize the information given. Your summary should be a full, well-connected paragraph. Underline the words you use from Chapter 6.

Income and Education

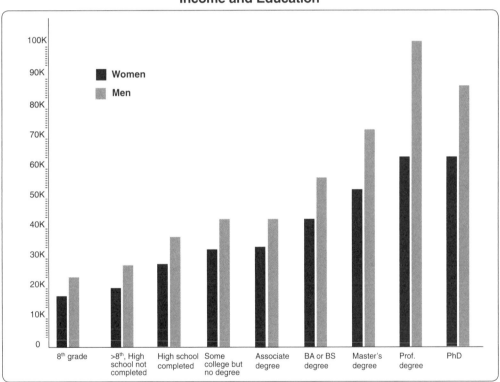

Note: Figures are for exercise purposes only. Not drawn from actual data.

Chapter 6: Links, Correlations, Happening Together

Quiz 2

I. Sentence Completion

Circle the best item to complete each sentence. Be careful. In some sentences both choices might be possible, but one is a better choice than the other.

1. In North America, the unusual weather *(to the degree that/associated with)* a strong El Niño includes heavy rains in California.

2. According to the principles of a philosophy called Huna, you will be happy with others only *(to the degree that/goes along with)* you are happy with yourself.

3. Branch-like channels on some Martian mountainsides *(imply/infer)* that a liquid, perhaps water, once flowed on the planet's surface.

4. Constant pressure from reporters and photographers *(goes along with/is characteristic of)* being famous.

5. Through most of recorded history, madness has been *(linked to/implied by)* a disease known as rabies, which attacks and destroys the human nervous system.

II. Paraphrasing

Use the best item from the list to rephrase each statement. Change the form of the item if necessary to fit the grammar of the sentence. You may also change words in the sentence itself. Do not change the meaning of the original statement. Use each item from the list only once.

accompany	imply
characteristic of	in conjunction with
correlation	

1. New studies show a link between the ease of voter registration and the number of people who actually vote.

   _____

   _____

2. Whenever the animals and plants of a certain area are isolated from outsiders, new species peculiar to the cut-off region are likely to develop.

   _____

   _____

3. If someone is a successful manager, he or she probably speaks honestly to other people.

   _____

   _____

4. The Casnovian Philosophical Society will have its annual meeting at the same time and in the same city as that of its parent organization, the North American Philosophical Society.

   _____

   _____

5. If a politician has a huge amount of money in a campaign fund, I assume that something dishonest or corrupt is going on.

   _____

   _____

III. Applying the Vocabulary

Using at least five words from Chapter 6, summarize the information given. Your summary should be a full, well-connected paragraph. Underline the words you use from Chapter 6.

Public Thoroughfares and Prosperity

City, Town, etc.	Barker City	New Bohemia	Scottville	Yakiva	Dry Cloud	Dordt
Year(s) of peak prosperity	1996	1890, 1973	1891, 1962	1998	1905, 1971	1897, 1971
Railroad built through town	1887	1887	1888	1890	1892	1894
Railroad stop established	NA	1902	1888	NA	1902	1894
Railroad stop closed	NA	NA	1982	NA	1910	NA
Freeway constructed	1959	1959	1959	1960	1961	1963
Freeway interchange opened	NA	1970	1959	1995	1968	1968
Freeway interchange closed	NA	NA	NA	2002	2002	NA

Chapter 6: Links, Correlations, Happening Together

Quiz 3: Collocations and Common Phrases

I. Collocations and Common Phrases

Fill in each blank with the best item from the list. Not every item from the list will be used. Some items may be used more than once.

are	mutual respect	risk
character	people	side effects
children	plan	to
evidence	positive	with
is	of	
meanings	offer	

1. Several researchers have found a _____ correlation between a child's even temperament and the amount of parental punishment he or she received during the pre-school years.

2. Effective psychotherapy implies _____ between the patient and the therapist.

3. The prosecutor had more than enough evidence to link the defendant _____ the murders.

4. When reading or listening, people infer _____ beyond what is actually said or written.

5. Unfortunately, a substantial _____ goes along with any investment meant to yield exceptional returns.

6. _____ like a dry mouth often accompany the use of netrozoluine and other anti-depressant drugs.

7. The fingerprints were not very convincing because they occurred in conjunction _____ no other physical evidence.

8. Sudden poverty, perhaps brought on by a health problem or an expensive divorce, _____ characteristic _____ America's working poor.

9. In many cities, public schools _____ associated _____ drugs, weapons, bullies, and uninspired teachers.

II. Paraphrasing

Using the item in parentheses, rephrase each statement. Change the form of the item if necessary to fit the grammar of the sentence. You may also change words in the sentence itself. Do not change the meaning of the original item.

1. *(link)* A tuberculosis epidemic coincided with the worldwide spread of Human Immunodeficiency Virus (HIV).

   _____

   _____

2. *(infer)* The pattern of plant growth along the dunes suggests that a strong, steady northwest wind blows off the lake.

   _____

   _____

3. *(imply)* If an east African society places great value on the ownership of cattle, anthropologists expect some Bantu influence on that society.

   _____

   _____

4. *(accompany)* The dreaded plague that swept Europe in the Middle Ages was called the bubonic plague because of the buboes—inflammations of the lymph nodes—that appeared in infected persons.

_____

_____

5. *(correlation)* Larger companies tend to pay higher salaries to their senior executives.

_____

_____

III. Applying the Vocabulary

Using at least five words from Chapter 6, summarize the reading passage "Investigating the Relationship of Biology to Emotion" (see the Appendix, pages 202–3). A beginning sentence for the summary has been written for you to help you get started. Use your own words. Underline the words you use from Chapter 6.

Summary

Research into the effects of brain chemicals on emotion has yielded some interesting observations and some effective medications.

Chapter 6: Links, Correlations, Happening Together

Quiz 4: Key Words and Related Word Forms

I. Fill in the Blanks

Fill in each blank with the best item from the list. Change the form of the item if necessary to fit the grammar of the sentence. You may also change words in the sentence itself. Use each item only once.

associate	implicit
characterized	to the degree that
going along with	

1. The decline of the League of Nations _____ the rise of European fascism in the 1930s.

2. Desert climates are _____ by a large difference between daytime and nighttime temperatures.

3. Most listeners _____ the orchestral composer John Cage with a musical style that combines dissonance and silence.

4. Until reaching its freezing point, a fluid's volume decreases _____ its temperature is lowered.

5. The patient's right to ask for a pain-killing drug is _____ in any case of invasive surgery.

II. Paraphrasing

Use the best item from the list to rephrase each statement. Change the form of the item if necessary to fit the grammar of the sentence. You may also change words in the sentence itself. Do not change the meaning of the original statement. Use each item from the list only once.

accompanying	inference
correlative	link
implication	

1. Some female birds apparently associate a male's coloring with his capacity to breed successfully.

   _____

   _____

2. Professor Ghazal's astrophysical research showed that old stars produce a stronger "stellar wind" than young stars do.

   _____

   _____

3. Oncologists have established a connection between intestinal cancer and such personality traits as excessive worrying.

   _____

   _____

4. In the 1970s, Professor Ilda Thorvald of Bergstrom University taught that a person could not be both male and feminist.

_____

_____

5. The United Nations report focused on the economic diversity in seven countries and on the fact that these economies were also very stable.

_____

_____

III. Applying the Vocabulary

The map shows where a European people called the Vriesians settled when they immigrated to the United States during four periods of history. It also shows some data about religion, education, and other aspects of Vriesian life in the United States. What connections do you see? Using at least five words from Chapter 6, describe some of those connections. Your answer should be a full, well-connected paragraph about 100 words long. Underline the words you use from Chapter 6.

Vriesians in the Northeast and Midwest

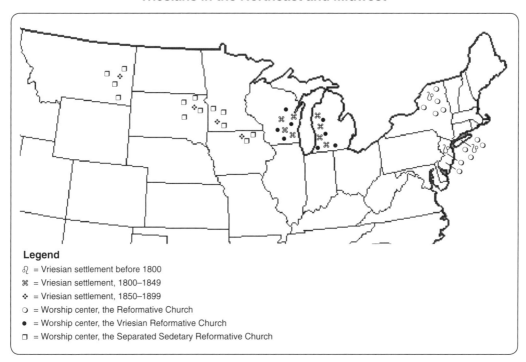

Legend

Ω = Vriesian settlement before 1800
⌘ = Vriesian settlement, 1800–1849
❖ = Vriesian settlement, 1850–1899
○ = Worship center, the Reformative Church
● = Worship center, the Vriesian Reformative Church
◻ = Worship center, the Separated Sedetary Reformative Church

Thinking about Metaphors

Fill in the middle column with concepts that, in your native language, fit each description in the left-hand column. Write in your native language, if necessary, and then translate into English. In the right-hand column, write any concepts that you know of that, in English usage, fit each description at the left. Some concepts have been supplied to get you started.

	In My Native Language	In English
Things that can sprout from some basic condition, like leaves from a plant		difficulties attitudes or feelings
Things that can come into being from a larger source, like small rivers branching off from a larger one		beliefs musical styles
Things that can give birth to other things		economic activity (gives birth to wealth) advertising (gives birth to sales)

133

Things that can move other things forward		lack of parental discipline (encourages bad behavior in children) a well-balanced diet (advances a person's health)

Chapter 7: Causes and Effects

Additional Vocabulary Quiz

I. Categorizing

Cross out the one item in each set that—*in its meaning as used in Chapter 7*—fits most poorly into the category. Be prepared to give reasons for your choice if your teacher asks you to.

Example:

Making schedules: ~~clock~~   calendar   appointment

<u>Note</u>: *Clock* is not totally unrelated to the category, but the other two terms relate more strongly.

Vocabulary related to:

1.	**Becoming worse:**	deterioration	devaluation	opaque
2.	**Worker-management relations:**	funding	labor unrest	strike
3.	**Sickness:**	bacterium	infect	speechless
4.	**Crime:**	corruption	gang	slash-and-burn
5.	**Factories:**	automate	colonialism	quality control

II. Paraphrasing

Use the best item from the list to rephrase each statement. Change the form of the item if necessary to fit the grammar of the sentence. You may also change words in the sentence itself. Do not change the meaning of the original statement. Use each item from the list only once.

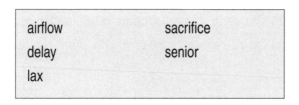

airflow	sacrifice
delay	senior
lax	

1. To properly ventilate a room, you should open at least two windows—one across the room from the other.

   _____

   _____

2. No matter what I have to give up, I will make sure my children get a good education.

   _____

   _____

3. Because security was not tight enough, thieves got into the building and stole three valuable works of art.

   _____

   _____

4. Mr. Trent has worked here longer than anyone else on the staff.

   _____

   _____

5. Because of bad weather, Flight 841 could not take off on time.

_____

_____

III. Applying the Vocabulary

Using at least five additional vocabulary words from Chapter 7 (see page 218 of *BAV*), answer one of the questions that follows the reading. Your answer should be one or two full, well-connected paragraphs (150–200 words). Underline the words you use from Chapter 7.

- -

A public official is corrupt if he or she uses power in order to get extra personal wealth or privileges to which the job does not entitle the official. For example, a police officer who stops a motorist for speeding and then accepts a $20 bribe for not writing a ticket is engaging in small-time corruption. More seriously, a law-enforcement official might secretly accept payment from a business group in exchange for the official's silence about some illegal activity by the business. Corruption can also be very subtle. A legislator might accept vacations or fine dinners or hard-to-get sports tickets from some business or organization that asks the legislator for nothing in return. Often, however, the "gift" goes to a lawmaker in a position to influence legislation affecting the donor's interests. After being treated so well by Company A or Political Group B, the lawmaker is likely to vote in a way that advances their interests—which are not necessarily the interests of most people who elected the legislator.

- -

Comment on one of the following issues related to corruption:

- *If you have personally witnessed corruption by a public official, tell the story of what you witnessed.*

- *Choose a country you know well (the United States, a country where you have lived, etc.). Does corruption exist among public officials in that country? How do you know whether it does or not?*

- *Why do public officials become corrupt?*

- *What is the best way to prevent corruption among public officials?*

Chapter 7: Causes and Effects

Quiz 1

I. Fill in the Blanks

Fill in each blank with the best item from the list. Change the form of the item if necessary to fit the grammar of the sentence. Use each item from the list only once.

be responsible for	provoke
generate	stem from
promote	

1. Learning a second or third language may _____ the development of new neural pathways in several parts of the brain.

2. The sun's UVB rays, the "tanning" rays, _____ most sunburns.

3. The operation of an integrated electrical circuit consumes a tiny amount of energy and _____ only a tiny amount of heat.

4. Failure to face one's sadness after the death of a close relative can _____ a number of psychological problems.

5. Sarah believes that her neighborhood's health and vitality _____ the presence of a strong, successful public school.

II. Paraphrasing

Use the best item from the list to rephrase each statement. Change the form of the item if necessary to fit the grammar of the sentence. You may also change words in the sentence itself. Do not change the meaning of the original statement. Use each item from the list only once.

be blamed for	generate
derive from	led to
favor	

1. After Jim Stadler lost the election for county commissioner, he claimed that local television stations had unfairly given his opponent a lot of positive news coverage.

   _____

   _____

2. Stock market analysts have predicted that software companies will be more profitable next year than they recently have been.

   _____

   _____

3. Modern viewers misunderstand silent films from the early 20th century because many visual symbols from that era have lost their meaning.

   _____

   _____

4. On July 12, 1965, a leak from a chemical tank killed at least 73 people in Monakwah Valley.

   _____

   _____

5. The governor argued that his mistakes were really his advisers' fault, not his own.

_____

_____

III. Applying the Vocabulary

Using at least five words from Chapter 7, summarize the information given. Your summary should be a full, well-connected paragraph. Underline the words you use from Chapter 7.

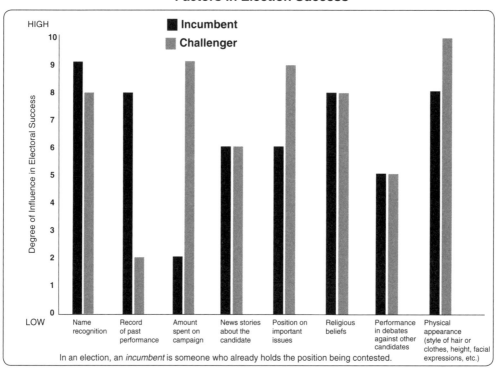

Factors in Election Success

Note: Figures are for exercise purposes only. Not drawn from actual data.

Chapter 7: Causes and Effects

Quiz 2

I. Sentence Completion

Circle the best item to complete each sentence. Be careful. In some sentences both choices might be possible, but one is a better choice than the other.

1. Even a minor injury to her legs will *(render/provoke)* her unable to participate in the triathlon.

2. The traffic jam *(led to/made)* John miss his afternoon appointment.

3. The yellow flames that rise from burning driftwood *(yield/are due to)* the element sodium soaked up by the wood from seawater.

4. Historically, longer-term bonds generally *(yield/promote)* higher interest rates than do short-term issues.

5. *(Generating/Leading to)* enthusiasm among certain church groups was a key element of Carl Dawge's campaign strategy.

II. Paraphrasing

Use the best item from the list to rephrase each statement. Change the form of the item if necessary to fit the grammar of the sentence. You may also change words in the sentence itself. Do not change the meaning of the original statement. Use each word from the list only once.

favor	render
generate	stem from
promote	

1. Sucralose, though about 600 times sweeter than sugar, does not contribute to tooth decay.

   _____

   _____

2. Even very small errors in the measurement of current weather conditions can make long-term forecasts undependable.

   _____

   _____

3. His timidity came not from an unwillingness to express himself but from painful embarrassment over his speech problems.

   _____

   _____

4. Richard's painful divorce caused his family and his ex-wife's family to distrust each other.

   _____

   _____

5. The weather on the eastern seaboard, especially when onshore winds are brisk but not too strong, is often ideal for kite-flying.

_____

_____

III. Applying the Vocabulary

In a recent survey, 500 people who said they would never visit the Republic of Visigothia were asked to state their reasons. This pie chart shows their responses. Using at least five words from Chapter 7, summarize the information given. Your summary should be a full, well-connected paragraph. Underline the words you use from Chapter 7.

Reasons Given for Not Wanting to Visit Visigothia

- Other 4%
- Language problems 7%
- Unsafe 37%
  - crime 13%
  - disease 14%
  - attacks by rebels 10%
- Unfriendly people 15%
- Bad weather 16%
- Too expensive 21%

Note: Figures are for exercise purposes only. Not drawn from actual data.

Chapter 7: Causes and Effects

Quiz 3: Collocations and Common Phrases

I. Collocations and Common Phrases

Fill in each blank with the best item from the list. Not every item on the list will be used. Some items may be used more than once.

among	in	resentment
development	income	tends to
expertise	jealousy	to
from	primarily	trouble
has been	reaction	

1. Some politicians are clearly more interested in generating _____ for themselves than in doing what's best for the nation.

2. Ethnic profiling by the police yields _____ among targeted groups in the community and does not lead to the more efficient apprehension of criminals.

3. By talking about her expensive birthday presents, the little girl was trying to provoke _____ among her friends.

4. A new bridge to Barron's Island promoted the _____ of several luxury resorts along the beaches.

5. The transportation department has predicted that a rise in three-car families may lead _____ parking problems by the end of the decade.

6. Ironically, rainy spring weather in western forests _____ favor severe fires later in the year, after the rain-nourished underbrush has dried out.

7. His expertise in Chinese language derives _____ many years of residence in the coastal cities of the mainland.

8. The large middle class in America is _____ responsible for decades of unremarkable, middle-of-the-road government policies.

9. The storm _____ blamed for at least three deaths.

10. _____ promoting development in sub-Saharan Africa, the United Kingdom hopes to discourage social upheaval.

II. Paraphrasing

Using the item in parentheses, rephrase each statement. Change the form of the item if necessary to fit the grammar of the the sentence. You may also change words in the sentence itself. Do not change the meaning of the original statement.

1. *(lead to)* The senator hopes that a visit to his home state will help him see what his constituents' real needs are and better represent them in Washington.

    _____

    _____

2. *(stem from)* The $1 million in fines levied against Arthur Jones result from his conviction for illegally altering the financial records of his trucking business.

    _____

    _____

3. (provoke) The manager deliberately angered the employees in order to cause them to strike.

    _____

    _____

4. *(be due to)* Anomalies in magnetic pressure, gas pressure, and gas temperature probably all contribute to the formation of sunspots.

_____

_____

5. *(be responsible for)* More than a million Cambodians died in the 1970s because of the bizarre, heartless policies enforced by the Khmer Rouge government.

_____

_____

III. Applying the Vocabulary

Using at least five words from Chapter 7, summarize the reading passage "Analysts Ponder Factors in BelSync's Profitable Quarter" (see the Appendix, pages 204–5). A beginning sentence for the summary has been written for you to help you get started. Use your own words. Underline the words you use from Chapter 7.

Summary

Speculation about the causes of BelSync's recent profits has ranged widely.

Chapter 7: Causes and Effects

Quiz 4: Key Words and Related Word Forms

I. Fill in the Blanks

Fill in each blank with the best item from the list. Change the form of the item if necessary to fit the grammar of the sentence. Use each item only once.

be responsible for	provoke
derive from	render
favor	

1. Much of modern western culture _____ earlier cultures in southwest Asia.

2. The makers of a spray called SafeGas claimed that it could _____ an attacker helpless within three seconds.

3. A federal appeals court ruled that two police officers _____ the death of a robbery suspect who died in the North County Jail in 2005.

4. Because King Marco and Queen Vera had no children, their death _____ a vigorous power struggle among several of their nieces and nephews.

5. The lack of natural predators such as wolves _____ the growth of the deer population.

II. Paraphrasing

Use the best item from the list to rephrase each statement. Change the form of the item if necessary to fit the grammar of the the sentence. You may also change words in the sentence itself. Do not change the meaning of the original statement. Use each item from the list only once.

be blamed for	promote
be due to	yield
generate	

1. The teacher believed that the new textbook was not likely to work very well for most students.

   _____

   _____

2. An increase in the recruiting budget should help make the university's student body more diverse.

   _____

   _____

3. A defective engine part called an O-ring almost certainly caused the space-shuttle disaster.

   _____

   _____

4. For more than half a century, each generation in Tejatria has been better nourished than its parents, which probably accounts for a steady rise in the average height of the population.

   _____

   _____

5. Made-for-TV movies are profitable for television companies because their production costs are relatively low.

   _____

   _____

III. Applying the Vocabulary

Using at least five words from Chapter 7, summarize the information given. Your summary should be a full, well-connected paragraph. Underline the words you use from Chapter 7.

- -

Aggressive Behavior

Aggressive behavior can be defined as a set of actions that initiate conflict, either physical or verbal. The aggressor starts a fight, and the defender (even one whose actions are stronger or more violent) reacts to the offense. Countless factors feed into aggressive behavior, and many aggressive acts have more than one genesis. For example, someone who has a slight imbalance in brain chemicals might not normally be aggressive, but the imbalance may make him or her more prone to start a conflict while drinking alcohol in a hot, crowded room after a bad day at work.

- -

This table lists a few possible factors in aggressive behavior.

Type of Factor	Examples	Comments
Biological or Chemical		
	excessive stimulation of the amygdala (a part of the brain)	Brain structure and chemistry are still poorly understood. These causes are hypothetical at present.
	low levels of serotonin (a chemical that helps transmit signals in the brain)	
	drinking alcohol	Suppresses self-control mechanisms
	low blood-sugar levels	called hypoglycemia
	unusually high levels of testosterone (a hormone that adult male animals have in higher amounts than females or young males)	Aggression does not imply a connection between testosterone and violence. Aggressive behavior may include over-competitiveness.
Environmental		
	being raised among others who behave aggressively	Children who grow up seeing violent adult behavior may see it as a part of normal adulthood.
	excessive exposure to violence on television, in video games, etc.	Evidence is contradictory. Some studies find it very influential. Others do not.
	availability of guns, knives, or other weapons	
	heat, noise, crowding, or other tension-creating conditions	

Type of Factor	Examples	Comments
Emotional		
	frustration at the apparently unreasonable actions of others	
	anger	
	phobias (excessive fear of heights, being in small places, etc.)	Fears can trigger the "fight" response.
	feelings of inadequacy	Low self-esteem may prompt aggression to repel others.

Chapter 8: Permitting, Making Easier

Thinking about Metaphors

Fill in the middle column with concepts that, in your native language, fit each description in the left-hand column. Write in your native language, if necessary, and then translate into English. In the right-hand column, write any concepts that you know of that, in English usage, fit each description at the left. Some concepts have been supplied to get you started.

	In My Native Language	In English
Things that can let other things through		rules or laws people in positions of authority
Things that can be unusually soft		a parent's treatment of a child courts of law
Things that can travel a road		hiring or firing an employee (a process) the Civil Rights Movement (a social force)

153

Obligations you can sometimes avoid before they start		paying taxes serving in the army

Chapter 8: Permitting, Making Easier

Additional Vocabulary Quiz

I. Categorizing

Cross out the one item in each set that—*in its meaning as used in Chapter 8*—fits most poorly into the category. Be prepared to give reasons for your choice if your teacher asks you to.

Example:

Making schedules: ~~clock~~   calendar   appointment

Note: *Clock* is not totally unrelated to the category, but the other two terms relate more strongly.

Vocabulary related to:

1. **Air movement:**	circulation	transition	vents
2. **A violent storm:**	enforce	toll	victim
3. **Leaving a job:**	evaporation	resignation	retirement
4. **A trial in court:**	convicted	sentence	upbringing
5. **Military forces:**	criticize	deployment	troops

II. Paraphrasing

Use the best item from the list to rephrase each statement. Change the form of the item if necessary to fit the grammar of the sentence. You may also change words in the sentence itself. Do not change the meaning of the original statement. Use each item from the list only once.

cash flow	market economy
cut costs	upbringing
interview	

1. Bezickas Construction Co. is looking for new equipment that can make it less expensive for them to build a house.

   _____

   _____

2. He addresses everyone as Sir or Ma'am because he grew up in a small southern town.

   _____

   _____

3. In an economy that features very little regulation of big business, small businesses have to be very lucky to survive.

   _____

   _____

4. The mayor has set aside some time to talk to us at 4:00 tomorrow afternoon.

   _____

   _____

5. Because customers have been so late in paying us, we haven't had enough money on hand to pay our own bills.

_____

_____

III. Applying the Vocabulary

A recent survey investigated the strategies being contemplated by executives of ailing U.S. firms. The chart shows the relative popularity of certain strategies. Using at least five additional vocabulary words from Chapter 8 (see page 218 of *BAV*), explain the information given. Underline the words you use from Chapter 8.

How Sick Companies Plan to Get Healthy Again

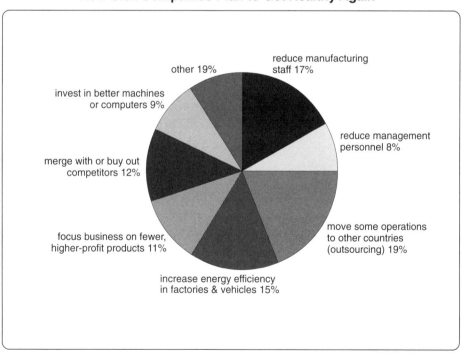

Note: Figures are for exercise purposes only. Not drawn from actual data.

Chapter 8: Permitting, Making Easier

Quiz 1

I. Fill in the Blanks

Fill in each blank with the best item from the list. Change the form of the item if necessary to fit the grammar of the sentence. Use each item from the list only once.

ease	lenient
excuse	permit
facilitate	

1. High-density lipoprotein is sometimes called good cholesterol because it

   _____ the removal of harmful compounds from the body.

2. The Borgman Center for Mental Health does not _____ patients for missing

   appointments, a policy that helps patients strengthen their memory skills.

3. The girl's mother would not _____ her to have her ear pierced in several

   places.

4. For recent immigrants, the help of bilingual social-service officials can _____

   the difficult transition into a new life in a new country.

5. If one parent is overly strict and the other is overly _____, children have

   difficulty knowing how to behave.

II. Paraphrasing

Use the best item from the list to rephrase each statement. Change the form of the item if necessary to fit the grammar of the sentence. You may also change words in the sentence itself. Do not change the meaning of the original statement. Use each item from the list only once.

allow	consent
approval	exempt
clear the way for	

1. Diet pills made from herbs are sold without any formal review by the Food and Drug Administration.

   _____

   _____

2. Having been re-elected, the governor wrongly assumed that she was free to pursue whatever policies she liked.

   _____

   _____

3. The riders stopped at several grassy spots on the dry plateau to let their horses graze.

   _____

   _____

4. U.S. citizens who live in a foreign country and meet certain other requirements do not have to pay U.S. income taxes.

   _____

   _____

5. Unless the U.S. Senate agrees, no presidential nominee can be appointed to the Supreme Court.

   _____

   _____

III. Applying the Vocabulary

Using at least five words from Chapter 8, summarize the information given. Your summary should be a full, well-connected paragraph. Underline the words you use from Chapter 8.

Conditions Favorable for the Formation of Tornadoes

Condition	Comments
Great temperature difference between surface temperatures (warm) and air at higher levels (cool)	An essential condition. Without this, updrafts cannot form.
Strong updrafts	
Contast between moist air to the east and dry air to the west	Especially in Texas and Oklahoma, a dry line is a factor in the formation of tornadoes. The line defines the boundary of an air mass with high humidity and one with low humidity, even though temperatures on both sides of the line are about the same.
Different wind directions at different layers of the atmosphere	Absolutely essential. Without this difference, no rotation can form in a thunderstorm.
A strong jet stream (air moving very fast) at about 35,000 feet in the atmosphere	Not necessary, but helpful in tornado formation.
Flat topography on the surface (water, grasslands, etc.)	This is why tornadoes do not often occur in mountains and rarely hit the center of a large city.
Surface temperatures between about 55° and 95° degrees Fahrenheit (F)	Lower than 55° F, the surface temperature is unlikely to contrast sharply with slightly higher air. Above 95° F, surface air is unlikely to be humid enough to support the formation of storms.
Location in the temperate zones of the earth—between the polar regions and the tropics	Not necessary. Tornadoes in equatorial regions are possible. Tornadoes in the Arctic and Antarctic are virtually unknown.

Chapter 8: Permitting, Making Easier

Quiz 2

I. Sentence Completion

Circle the best item to complete each sentence. Be careful. In some sentences both choices might be possible, but one is a better choice than the other.

1. Children are loud and annoying at times, but adults have to be tolerant and *(consent/permit)* them to act their age.

2. If the government of Vetronia really wants to *(permit/remove obstacles to)* outside investment, it must aggressively punish any official who demands a bribe from a businessperson.

3. It is unlikely that Congress would ever *(promote/allow)* government-backed bonds to fail.

4. If children get a little dirty while playing outside, parents should be *(lenient/permissive)*; the exposure to backyard bacteria helps strengthen a child's immune system.

5. Every young man in South Korea is required to serve in the military, and very few are *(approved for/exempt from)* the obligation, even for serious health reasons.

II. Paraphrasing

Use the best item from the list to rephrase each statement. Change the form of the item if necessary to fit the grammar of the sentence. You may also change words in the sentence itself. Do not change the meaning of the original statement. Use each item from the list only once.

approval	lenient
ease	permit
facilitate	

1. If the Republic of Batang reforms its international trading practices, high-quality consumer goods from overseas could become more affordable to the average Batangian.

   _____

   _____

2. After a lengthy period of fasting (choosing to eat or drink very little), sudden resumption of a solid-food diet is a painful mistake. Drinking only juices for a while can reduce one's discomfort during the interim.

   _____

   _____

3. The top two tennis players in the world refused to be tested for drugs and were denied places in this weekend's Bellwood Invitational Tournament.

   _____

   _____

4. Prisoners who could provide guards with valuable information were treated less harshly than most.

    _____

    _____

5. Even people who feel alienated from mainstream society feel a sense of belonging if they get the respect of other outcasts.

    _____

    _____

III. Applying the Vocabulary

Using at least five words from Chapter 8, summarize the information given. Your summary should be a full, well-connected paragraph. Underline the words you use from Chapter 8.

Some Genetically Determined Features that Improve an Organism's Chances of Breeding

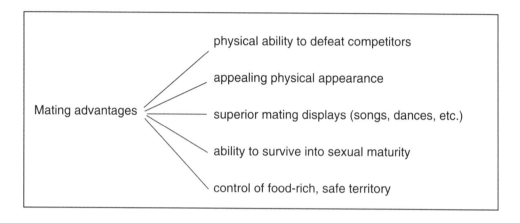

Mating advantages
- physical ability to defeat competitors
- appealing physical appearance
- superior mating displays (songs, dances, etc.)
- ability to survive into sexual maturity
- control of food-rich, safe territory

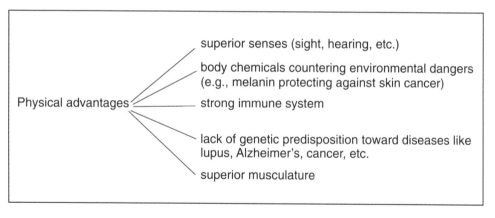

Physical advantages
- superior senses (sight, hearing, etc.)
- body chemicals countering environmental dangers (e.g., melanin protecting against skin cancer)
- strong immune system
- lack of genetic predisposition toward diseases like lupus, Alzheimer's, cancer, etc.
- superior musculature

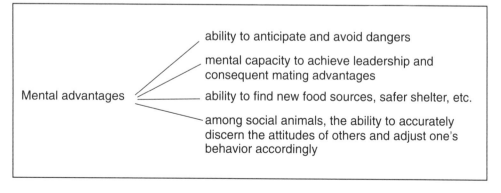

Mental advantages
- ability to anticipate and avoid dangers
- mental capacity to achieve leadership and consequent mating advantages
- ability to find new food sources, safer shelter, etc.
- among social animals, the ability to accurately discern the attitudes of others and adjust one's behavior accordingly

Chapter 8: Permitting, Making Easier

Quiz 3: Collocations and Common Phrases

I. Collocations and Common Phrases

Fill in each blank with the best item from the list. Not every item on the list will be used. Some items may be used more than once.

be	give	time
diagnosis	herself	treated
from	in	under
get	suffering	

1. The students prepared for the exams as thoroughly as _____ allowed.

2. A judge may refuse to accept a defendant's confession if it was obtained _____ circumstances where the police intimidated the suspect.

3. Children who are routinely excused _____ physical education classes do not get enough physical exercise.

4. In Tyrrhenian culture, mentally disabled criminals were _____ leniently because they were assumed to have no real understanding of their actions.

5. By signing this application, you _____ your consent for us to check your credit history.

6. Federal law says that medicines must _____ governmental approval before being marketed in the United States.

7. Negotiators from a few nations argued that, under the treaty, nuclear weapons should _____ exempt from international inspections.

8. The president had to excuse _____ from the formal dinner because her stomach was very upset.

9. In magnetic-resonance imaging (MRI) examinations, a liquid called a contrast can facilitate _____ by making certain tissues easier to see.

10. A hospice organization aims not to cure a patient but to ease _____ during his or her last few days before death.

II. Paraphrasing

Using the item in parentheses, rephrase each statement. Change the form of the item if necessary to fit the grammar of the sentence. You may also change words in the sentence itself. Do not change the meaning of the original statement.

1. *(allow)* In several religious traditions, the place of worship for women must be separate from that for men.

    _____

    _____

2. *(consent)* The corps commander said it would be all right for a tank battalion to race up the river valley toward the airport.

    _____

    _____

3. *(excuse)* Because Galbraith has to take his child to the hospital, he will be allowed to miss today's training session.

    _____

    _____

4. *(permissive)* Parenting practices that seem normal to one family might seem shockingly undisciplined to another.

_____

_____

5. *(exempt)* The new proposal would let logging companies cut roads through national forests, despite long-standing bans on any vehicle traffic through these areas.

_____

_____

III. Applying the Vocabulary

Using at least five words from Chapter 8, summarize the reading passage "Federal Power and States' Rights" (see the Appendix, pages 206–8). A beginning sentence for the summary has been written for you to help you get started. Use your own words. Underline the words you use from Chapter 8.

Summary

From the very earliest years of the republic, the United States has struggled to find the proper balance of power between the federal government and the states.

Chapter 8: Permitting, Making Easier

Quiz 4: Key Words and Related Word Forms

I. Fill in the Blanks

Fill in each blank with the best item from the list. Change the form of the item if necessary to fit the grammar of the sentence. Use each item only once.

allowance	exemption
consent	permit
excuse	

1. We'll hear several project-related reports at the end of the meeting, if time

   _____.

2. Prime Minister Robertson _____ to negotiations with his political rivals, but only if they all agreed to be searched for weapons before the meeting.

3. According to the laws of the Ferrugi Republic, a Ferrugian citizen gets an income tax _____ on any money earned in a foreign country.

4. The American Child Health Association says that a daily _____ of one hour of video game time per child should be the maximum in any household.

5. Lenny's chronic headaches are no _____ for his rude behavior at the office.

II. Paraphrasing

Use the best item from the list to rephrase each statement. Change the form of the item if necessary to fit the grammar of the sentence. You may also change words in the sentence itself. Do not change the meaning of the original statement. Use each item from the list only once.

consenting adults	make allowance for
facilitator	remove a barrier to
John Hancock	

1. Retaking the test and getting a higher score would make it a lot easier for Simon to be accepted into Zwingli University.

   _____

   _____

2. If two adults both want to have a romantic relationship, the government should not interfere.

   _____

   _____

3. The document isn't legal until you sign it.

   _____

   _____

4. Anyone who tries to predict prices in the future has to consider inflation, which is a general tendency for prices to rise.

   _____

   _____

5. I'm willing to help you and your brother discuss your differences, but I am not going to take any position about who's right and who's wrong.

_____

_____

III. Applying the Vocabulary

Using at least five words from Chapter 8, answer the question. Your answer should be a full, well-connected paragraph. Underline the words you use from Chapter 8.

- -

Visitors to the United States or Canada are often surprised by the amount of freedom teenagers enjoy. North American families, they believe, have lost control of their teenaged children and fail to protect them from bad influences. Do you agree that North American teens are too loosely controlled? Support your opinion with specific reasons or examples.

- -

Thinking about Metaphors

Fill in the middle column with concepts that, in your native language, fit each description in the left-hand column. Write in your native language and translate it into English. In the right-hand column, write any concepts that you know of that, in English usage, fit each description at the left. Some concepts have been supplied to get you started.

	In My Native Language	In English
Things that can "hang the air," like a leaf in the wind, for a while		breathing official privileges, such as a driver's license
Things that can be stopped or delayed if someone sees them coming		criticism an investigation
Things that can be prevented from moving forward, as if by a large tree fallen across a road		electrical signals vision

173

Things that can be tied up and prevented from moving, as if by a rope or string		immigration opportunities

Chapter 9: Stopping, Preventing

Additional Vocabulary Quiz

I. Categorizing

Cross out the one item in each set that—*in its meaning as used in Chapter 9*—fits most poorly into the category. Be prepared to give reasons for your choice if your teacher asks you to.

Example:

Making schedules: ~~clock~~   calendar   appointment

<u>Note</u>: *Clock* is not totally unrelated to the category, but the other two terms relate more strongly.

Vocabulary related to:

1. **Kinds of medicine:**   vaccine   aspirin   drug trafficking
2. **Possible results of a trial:** fine   injury   imprisonment
3. **Places:**   patrol   campus   mall
4. **Possible results of a tidal wave:** power outage   injury   amnesty
5. **Reactions to an offense:**   rage   outcry   swift

II. Paraphrasing

Use the best item from the list to rephrase each statement. Change the form of the item if necessary to fit the grammar of the sentence. You may also change words in the sentence itself. Do not change the meaning of the original statement. Use each item from the list only once.

appeal	overdue
collapse	talented
get under way	

1. I was supposed to submit my homework last Tuesday, but I haven't handed it in yet.

   _____

   _____

2. As the storm knocked down trees and power lines, the sheriff issued an urgent plea for everyone to stay indoors.

   _____

   _____

3. Jamie has a lot of natural writing ability, but she doesn't work very hard to develop it.

   _____

   _____

4. Okay. If I could have everyone's attention please, this meeting can get started.

   _____

   _____

5. Earthquakes that send horizontal waves through soft soil cause more buildings to fall down than other types of earthquakes.

_____

_____

III. Applying the Vocabulary

Using at least five additional vocabulary items from Chapter 9 (see pages 218–19 of *BAV*), answer one question that follows the reading. Your answer should be one or two paragraphs of 150–200 words. Underline the words you use from Chapter 9.

- -

In May 2004, a survey taken by CNN and *Money* magazine showed that, once again, the average cost of tuition at well-respected colleges and universities in the United States is rising at least twice as fast as overall prices (see *money.cnn.com/2004/05/18/pf/college/tuition_increases*). Tuition increases for the 2004–2005 academic year were expected to range between 4.5 percent and about 11 percent. Overall, inflation in the United States at the time of the survey was about 2.3 percent.

Comment on one of these aspects of college tuition costs:

- Why do the costs of college tuition rise so much faster than costs in general?

- What factors might stop the rise in tuition costs?

- Even in-state tuition at the University of Michigan cost more than $8,000 per year at the time the survey was taken. Is this a wise investment for the average student?

- How can students protect their personal finances from some of the adverse effects of tuition increases?

- -

Chapter 9: Stopping, Preventing

Quiz 1

I. Fill in the Blanks

Fill in each blank with the best item from the list. Change the form of the item if necessary to fit the grammar of the sentence. Use each item from the list only once.

block	prevent
deny	restrict
hinder	suspend

1. Ebola virus will spread rapidly unless officials can _____ infected people from having any contact with other people.

2. If a customer fails to pay for several months, the electric company might _____ that person its services until the bill is settled.

3. All along the border, a high cement wall totally _____ entrance to Grimaldia.

4. John's loss of a finger may _____ him, but he's a productive writer anyway.

5. We can keep this room secure if we _____ entry to only a few people.

6. Because he hit a teacher, Drake was _____ from school for a week.

II. Paraphrasing

Use the best item from the list to rephrase each statement. Change the form of the item if necessary to fit the grammar of the sentence. You may also change words in the sentence itself. Do not change the meaning of the original statement. Use each item from the list only once.

cease	forestall
deter	halt
forbid	restrain

1. My religion does not allow smoking or dancing.

   _____

   _____

2. Economic development in Barriaville is held back by a very poor road system and undependable electric power.

   _____

   _____

3. The best way to keep bullies from bothering you is to have a lot of friends who will support you.

   _____

   _____

4. The referee declared that the game had to stop because of a storm with frequent lightning.

_____

_____

5. My devotion to my family will never come to an end.

_____

_____

III. Applying the Vocabulary

Using at least five words from Chapter 9, summarize the information given. Your summary should be one or two full, well-connected paragraphs of 100–150 words. Except for technical terms, do not simply repeat the vocabulary you see in the reading. Underline the words you use from Chapter 9.

- -

Cold Fusion

Definitions

Artificial nuclear fusion: The forced joining of two atomic nuclei, usually to release the energy that had bound each into a separate unit. The only prominent example is the reaction that creates the explosive force of a hydrogen bomb.

Natural nuclear fusion: A similar process that takes place naturally, most notably the reactions that characterize the energy production of active stars, like the sun.

Cold fusion: Theoretically, a form of artificial nuclear fusion achieved at very low temperatures and pressures and producing a controlled flow of energy (unlike the explosive release of a hydrogen bomb).

Reasons Artificial Nuclear Fusion Is Not Used for Power Generation

- Creating the necessary temperatures and pressures is an energy-negative process that uses more energy than is produced.

- Reactions produced at such extremes of temperature and pressure are nearly impossible to control. Sudden bursts of energy can neither be used nor stored.

- Currently, fusion is enormously expensive.

A Moment of Excitement

In 1969, a pair of physicists named Pons and Fleischmann created a scientific stir by claiming to have produced controllable energy by fusing the nuclei of two atoms at very low pressure and temperature. They also claimed that the amount of energy derived from the fusion was greater than the amount used to create it. No such controlled, energy-positive technique had yet been discovered. If Pons and Fleischmann could be proved right, an economic revolution would occur. Clean, hydrogen-based energy would replace energy from "dirty" fuels like coal, oil, and uranium.

Factors Eventually Discrediting the Pons-Fleischmann Claims

- The experiments were not independently reproducible. Countless other scientists tried, but failed, to do what Pons and Fleischman claimed to have done.

- Pons and Fleischmann could not reproduce their own results in the presence of independent observers.

- No plausible explanation was presented for the results of the original experiment.

- The original reports of success were easily explained as wishful thinking.

Chapter 9: Stopping, Preventing

Quiz 2

I. Sentence Completion

Circle the best item to complete each sentence. Be careful. In some sentences both choices might be possible, but one is a better choice than the other.

1. The medicines known as SSRIs *(hinder/deny)* the absorption of serotonin, a brain chemical, so cells don't take up too much of it too quickly.

2. If Earth's climate changes, wine producers may have to *(cease/restrict)* growing their best grapes in California and move farther north.

3. Richfield Inc., might be able to *(deter/forestall)* financial trouble if it closes some factories soon.

4. When you're hiking and you see bear cubs, just *(suspend/halt)* where you're standing.

5. Security officers tried to *(forbid/restrain)* a young man who rushed toward the stage while shouting insults at the speaker.

II. Paraphrasing

Use the best item from the list to rephrase each statement. Change the form of the item if necessary to fit the grammar of the sentence. You may also change words in the sentence itself. Do not change the meaning of the original statement. Use each item from the list only once.

blocked	forbid
deny	restricted
deter	

1. In the United States, no-cost medical treatment is only for extremely poor people and only in emergencies.

   _____

   _____

2. The Democratic Party tried hard to bring the bill to the Senate for a vote, but Senator Sterns successfully kept it from being voted on.

   _____

   _____

3. Most countries do not allow visitors to bring in fruits or vegetables from other countries.

   _____

   _____

4. To get information from the prisoners, soldiers would not let them have water, food, or sleep.

   _____

   _____

5. Olympic gymnast Leva Fedova had a cold and fever, but that didn't stop her from competing.

III. Applying the Vocabulary

Using at least five words from Chapter 9, summarize the information given. Your summary should be a full, well-connected paragraph. Underline the words you use from Chapter 9.

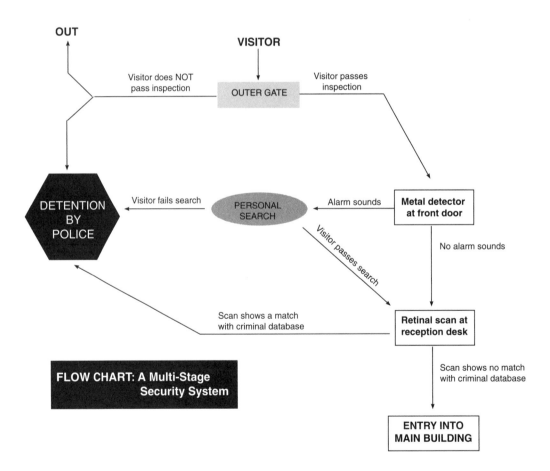

FLOW CHART: A Multi-Stage Security System

Chapter 9: Stopping, Preventing

Quiz 3: Collocations and Common Phrases

I. Collocations and Common Phrases

Fill in each blank with the best item from the list. Not every item on the list will be used. Some items may be used more than once.

are	getting	the invasion
call	in	to
desist	indefinitely	
from	myself	

1. The popular new Duluth Diet restricts a person _____ a total of 5,000 calories per day.

2. Presidential aides _____ forbidden _____ talk to the press about the president's family.

3. Only strong regulations by federal agencies restrain big companies _____ cheating consumers.

4. In late 1942, it seemed like nothing could deter Adolf Hitler _____ his drive to conquer all of Europe.

5. Ben joined a therapy group to prevent his beer-drinking _____ _____ out of control.

6. According to the court order, the construction company draining the wetlands had to cease and _____ until an environmental study was done.

7. Arguments between brothers and sisters are natural, but parents should _____ them _____ a halt if there's any shouting or hitting.

8. After being caught driving drunk three times, Alfred had his driver's license suspended _____.

9. I felt like telling Dr. Hendon that he was incompetent and shouldn't be practicing medicine, but I restrained _____.

10. The destruction of five bridges across the Loos River forestalled _____ _____.

II. Paraphrasing

Using the item in parentheses, rephrase each statement. Change the form of the item if necessary to fit the grammar of the sentence. You may also change words in the sentence itself. Do not change the meaning of the original statement.

1. *(suspend)* Because so many people are going out of town for the holiday, we should not have any more rehearsals until mid-January.

   _____

   _____

2. *(hinder)* I close my office door because the loud chatter of some colleagues keeps me from working as efficiently as I can.

   _____

   _____

3. *(prevent)* I don't really want my daughter to spend time with Jason, but I don't know how to stop them without alienating her.

_____

_____

4. *(restrict)* The library limits the number of CDs you can take out. You can't take anymore than three at one time.

_____

_____

5. *(deny)* Because we got a huge new order, the management of our factory would not let anyone take vacation days from May 12 to May 30.

_____

_____

III. Applying the Vocabulary

Using at least five words from Chapter 9, summarize the reading passage "Some Defenses against Disease" (see the Appendix, pages 209–10). A beginning sentence for the summary has been written for you to help you get started. Use your own words. Underline the words you use from Chapter 9.

Summary

The immune system, including the complement part of the system, provides impressive protection against illness.

Chapter 9: Stopping, Preventing

Quiz 4 : Key Words and Related Word Forms

I. Fill in the Blanks

Fill in each blank with the best item from the list. Change the form of the item if necessary to fit the grammar of the sentence. Use each item from the list only once.

cease	restraints
denial	restriction
forbidden	

1. The United Nations declared that holding prisoners for long periods without a trial is a _____ of their basic rights.

2. We have a saying, "If there are no _____ on the behavior of the young, no one lives to become old."

3. A delegation of high-level diplomats begged the king to _____ his preparations for war.

4. Each of Zachary's children received an inheritance of $100,000, but with the _____ that each had to donate a tenth of it to charity.

5. The holy temples were _____ territory, and anyone but a priest would be killed for entering them.

II. Paraphrasing

Use the best item from the list to rephrase each statement. Change the form of the items if necessary to fit the grammar of the sentence. You may also change words in the sentence itself. Do not change the meaning of the original statement. Use each item from the list only once.

ceaseless	hindrance
deterrent effect	suspension of disbelief
forestall	

1. Some hydrologists say there's no way to keep the Aral Sea from drying up entirely.

   _____

   _____

2. I was kept awake all night by the endless barking of a neighbor's dog.

   _____

   _____

3. For some girls, going to an all-girl high school removes a condition that keeps them from studying their best.

   _____

   _____

4. Fantasy movies can work well if the audience achieves a certain temporary willingness to accept the unbelievable.

   _____

   _____

5. For many years, the United States has relied on the fact that its nuclear weapons discourage enemies from attacking.

_____

_____

III. Applying the Vocabulary

Using at least five words from Chapter 9, answer the question. Your answer should be a full, well-connected paragraph of about 100 words. Underline the words you use from Chapter 9.

- -

Sociologists sometimes speak of a social underclass—a group of people who, generation after generation, remain poor, undereducated, and unaccepted by mainstream society. Such groups can be found in almost every society. Explain some of the factors that prevent an underclass from improving their conditions.

- -

APPENDIX: Readings for Quizzes

Chapter 1, Quiz 3 (page 34)

Taxonomy

Among the fundamental principles of biological science is the concept of taxonomy, that living things can be classified according to their physical traits. Animals, for example, are so different from plants that they belong together in a distinct grouping, the Animal Kingdom. Those animals that have a spinal column are then further grouped together as the phylum Chordata, because this physical trait makes them so different from animals (such as insects) that do not have it. The ultimate classification, the species, is considered definitional—that is, it is the ultimate determination of whether individuals are biologically similar enough to interbreed and produce offspring that can also interbreed.

Some taxonomic terms are very familiar and have become part of ordinary conversation. A speaker of English who refers to *Homo sapiens* can legitimately expect the listener to know that this Latin phrase means "a human." Most often-used taxonomic terms follow the pattern shown in *Homo sapiens*—a term for genus (e.g., *Homo*) followed by a term for species (e.g., *sapiens*). A common mouse is *Mus musculus*, while the kind of rat usually used in laboratory experiments is *Rattus norvegicus*. Despite their similar appearance, a rat and a mouse do not belong to the same genus, much less the same species.

A wolf is *Canis lupus*, while a dog is *Canis familiaris*. The obvious similarities between wolves and dogs reflect their membership in the genus *Canis*, but their differences are significant enough for them to be placed in separate species.

The taxonomic system currently used is essentially the one devised by the Swedish botanist Carolus Linnaeus (also known as Karl von Linné) in the middle of the 18th century. It is deeper than popular two-word terms like *Canis lupus* might suggest. The wolf belongs not only to a genus and a species but to many larger groups as well:

Kingdom: Animalia (animals)

Phylum: Chordata (vertebrates)

Class: Mammalia (mammals)

Subclass: Eutheria (placental mammals, as opposed to egg-laying mammals)

Order: Carnivora (meat-eaters)

Family: Canidae (the dog family)

Genus: *Canis* (modern dog-like creatures, such as wolves and coyotes)

Species: *lupus* (wolf)

By working backward through this system from *lupus* to *animalia*, one can see ever-larger groups to which an individual belongs. The Linnaean system of taxonomy was devised long before the genetic makeup of individuals was known, yet modern DNA analysis generally supports this classification scheme.

Chapter 2, Quiz 3 (page 53)

What Is, or Is Not, Europe?

Defining the boundaries of Europe has never been easy. Traditionally, Europe has been deemed to consist of:

1. All the lands east of the Atlantic Ocean and west of a line running from the Ural Mountains in Russia to the northwestern shores of the Caspian Sea.

2. All the lands south of the Arctic Ocean and north of a line running from the western shore of the Caspian along the Caucusus Mountains and roughly midway through the Black Sea, the Bosporus, and the Mediterranean Sea to the middle of the Strait of Gibraltar between Spain and Morocco.

3. Certain islands beyond these arbitrary lines, including Great Britain, Ireland, and Iceland in the northwest and Malta and Cyprus in the southeast.

This arbitrary set of dividing lines has created some political oddities. A small part of Turkey lies in Europe, while most of it is considered part of Asia. Turkey's largest city, Istanbul, is partly in each continent. Cyprus, which is only about 30 miles from the Asian part of Turkey, is unofficially split between a Turkish-controlled north and an officially independent, but culturally Greek, south. Russia is divided at the Urals, but the decidedly European culture of Moscow and St. Petersburg has a firm hold on decidedly Asian lands all the way to Sakhalin Island and the Kamchatka Peninsula. Iceland, an independent nation, is considered part of Europe, even though it is almost twice as far from Europe as from Greenland, which is a part of North America.

Iceland illustrates the difficulty of defining Europe in geological terms. As evidenced by its constant volcanic activity, Iceland lies right on the line where the Eurasian Plate of the earth's crust meets the North American Plate. Geologically only about half of Iceland is in Europe. Tectonic geology in the Mediterranean is very complex, with the Eurasian Plate sliding westward, while the African plate slides east. Most of Europe's earthquakes and volcanic activity occur along a line where the African Plate juts northward toward Sicily and the Balkans. The contact line then dives southward through the Greek islands before reaching a point just off Cyprus where the Eurasian, African, and Arabian plates all meet.

In a strict geological sense, a narrow strip of north Africa—the parts of Morocco and Algeria north of the High Atlas Mountains—should be called Europe because the mountains define the southern reach of the Eurasian Plate. Clearly, however, tectonic plates do not effectively define Europe. Tectonically, there is no Europe, only Eurasia. If mapmakers suddenly decided to use tectonic definitions for continents, Europe and most of Asia would fuse into one continent. The Arabian Peninsula would not be part of Asia anymore, because it lies on a separate plate. The same is true of India, southern Nepal, Pakistan, and Sri Lanka, while the easternmost parts of Siberia would be called part of North America.

Defining Europe in terms of culture or language is another fruitless pursuit. Even leaving aside the pernicious globalization of Western commercial products, European culture dominates nearly all of North America, South America, Australia, New Zealand, and countless other colonial or ex-colonial territories elsewhere. Linguistically, it would make sense to expel Hungary and Finland from Europe and annex Iran and India—because Hungarian and Finnish have less in common with most European tongues than do Hindi or Farsi.

The definition of Europe in political terms has become more difficult as the European Union (EU) has not only survived but prospered. Technically, Ireland could be considered more European than the United Kingdom, because Ireland has adopted the European currency, the euro, but Great Britain has not. Still, only a very fringey economist would dare speak of Britain, a member of the EU, as not being a part of Europe. As with nearly every other definitional criterion, Turkey presents a problem in defining Europe politically. Part of Turkey has always been considered part of the European landmass, giving Turkey a rationale for applying to the EU. If admitted, Turkey would extend Europe eastward among peoples (the rural Turks of inland Anatolia) who have little affinity with most of Europe, as it is traditionally conceived.

Chapter 3, Quiz 3 (page 72)

Generic Pharmaceuticals

Every state in the United States has some sort of law that allows pharmacists to fill medical prescriptions with a lower-cost generic drug instead of a higher-priced brand-name drug. Each state sets its own rules, but every law includes these provisions:

a. The patent on the original drug must have either expired or been surrendered by the pharmaceutical company that developed the drug.

b. The generic drug has to be just as medically effective as the original.

c. The generic drug has to be available in the same forms (pills, liquid, etc.) as the original.

d. The generic drug has to contain all the active ingredients of the original in the same proportions. In other words, there cannot be any significant chemical difference between the generic and the original.

e. The physician must write the prescription in a way that allows generics. If the physician specifies that a brand-name drug must be used, the pharmacist cannot legally give the patient a generic.

Many well-known drugs that seem relatively new to the public are, in fact, nearing the end of their patent lives and are soon to face competition from generics. The seemingly short life of the original patent is due mostly to a quirk in the patent process. The original product has patent protection for either 17 or 20 years (depending on when it was developed) from the date its developer applies for the patent—not from the date the patent is approved. Since patent approval often takes many years, the company may have only a few years left in which to market the drug. Extensions of the patent can partially restore lost time, but even extensions cannot change one huge limitation under the law: An original drug cannot be on the market under patent protection for more than 14 years.

With a large number of patents expiring, generic drug producers are raising the prices of their products because they believe the market will support higher prices. The generics may still be 15 percent cheaper than the originals, but consumers and health insurance companies had been used to savings of up to 60 percent. The narrower price gap is actually encouraging a downward trend in the prices of brand-name drugs, whose manufacturers hope to stay dominant in the market by bringing their price down to a level not far from that of the generics.

Chapter 4, Quiz 3 (page 91)

Unequal Distribution of Wealth

Capitalist societies assume that some people will be richer than others. The opportunity to use one's talents to avoid poverty and pursue wealth fuels the economy in a market-oriented system like that in the United States. Ideally, most of the wealth will be spread widely among a large, hard-working middle class. Few economists would advocate entrusting almost all of a nation's wealth to a tiny percentage of the population while poverty or near-poverty afflicts almost half of the people.

That, nonetheless, is an accurate picture of the United States wealth gap in the early 21st century. The wealthiest 10 percent of American households own more than 70 percent of all the wealth in the United States. At the other end of the spectrum, the poorest 40 percent of households own less than one-half of 1 percent of the wealth. Even this figure is deceivingly optimistic, since nearly half of this lower group owns nothing at all and is in fact deeply in debt.

The middle 50 percent of American households, the middle-class teachers and managers and service workers on whom a stable capitalist society supposedly rests, have little in common with the truly wealthy. Middle-class (and upper-middle-class) households control a paltry 28 percent of the nation's assets. A big gap separates even the top end of the upper-middle class from the rich. The second-richest 10 percent of American households have only about 8 percent of the nation's assets, small in comparison to the massive wealth in the 10 percent of households just above them. A middle-class family generally earns enough to provide the basics such as food and shelter, perhaps even an occasional nice vacation, but they live primarily by spending income, not by spending interest from investments. In other words, they have to do what nearly every financial counselor advises against.

The poorest 40 percent of American households cannot even identify with the basic comforts available to the middle class. Many among this lowest group are working poor, families with at least one member working full-time, but at very low wages. Typically, a household in this group owns very little, probably not even a house or car. More dangerously, they are likely to have no insurance against ordinary calamities—illness, disability, or even theft. This plurality of Americans is truly only one disease away from poverty.

The vast canyon between the rich and the rest represents a significant change in only a few decades. From the end of World War II until 1980, the middle class and even the poor increased their wealth by about the same percentage as did the rich. Differences among the groups were significant, but the rich had nothing like the virtual monopoly on resources that they have since acquired. Deregulation of industry, debilitating tax cuts, shameless give-aways of publicly owned natural resources (from land to timber and minerals), and welfare reform have each furthered the interests of the wealthy while making the poor easier to defraud or ignore.

Several conclusions can be drawn from the rapid widening of the wealth gap. One is that the rich, who are usually also the powerful, share very little experience of how most people live. The chances of granting high governmental priority to the problems of the poor are growing ever smaller Another is that the benefits of working for a living are no longer quite so attractive to those who used to receive support from public welfare programs. Welfare reform has put hundreds of thousands of Americans back to work, but in such low-paying jobs that they remain desperately poor.

Chapter 5, Quiz 3 (page 108)

Extreme Weather

The worst blizzard in history. The hottest summer on record. More rain than has ever fallen in a single day. The only tornado ever to strike the center of the city. In the late 20th century and early 21st, phrases such as these were ubiquitous in news about the weather. Was the weather on Earth actually becoming more extreme, or did it just seem to be? After all, modern systems of weather observation and measurement are far more sophisticated than those used even as recently as 30 years ago. Perhaps apparent changes in the weather are really just changes in our ability to measure the weather.

That's a tempting explanation, especially if one wants to discredit the concept of global climate change. The problem is that it runs contrary to the evidence.

Reliable weather records in most parts of the world go back about 150 years. Some records are older and some not as old, but with a 150-year sample, most localities have been able to establish a reasonable baseline—a depiction of normal weather, allowing for short-term ups and downs. At the beginning of this 150-year period, Earth was just emerging from "the Little Ice Age," a cool period that began in about 1200 CE and extended through the middle of the 19th century. Consequently, comparison of modern data with those of only, say, the 1860s or 1870s, might be considered unreasonable. The majority of record-keeping years, however, are considered consistent with average climatic conditions since about 8000 BCE. Consequently, 100-year averages provide a reliable tool for deciding whether a certain weather phenomenon is truly extreme. In locales with the most consistent records, this reliability is best.

For example, the tornado that struck downtown Salt Lake City on August 11, 1999, can be reliably called extreme. The Mormons who settled the area in the 1850s were excellent record-keepers, as are their ancestors. There is little doubt that tornadoes are extremely rare in Utah (perhaps two annually) and that downtown Salt Lake City is an extremely unlikely target. Nor is there very much doubt that the ten warmest years on record, worldwide, have all occurred since 1983. The range of observation stations in the mid-1800s was very wide, including all but the highest latitudes (the poles) and the highest mountains. Nor was it very difficult to measure air temperature. Enough reliable data could be collected from enough places. Modern observational techniques have had virtually no effect on the ability of meteorologists to calculate average air temperatures at the surface.

Logic dictates that a warmer world will also be a stormier one. As warmth increases, so does evaporation, one of the stages in the water cycle. Increased evaporation charges the atmosphere with more moisture, and the movement of water through the atmosphere increases the instability of air at various altitudes. The end result is an atmosphere primed not only to rain, but also to do so in the form of thunderstorms and hurricanes rather than gentle showers. While locales prone to receive greater precipitation will do so, the increased atmospheric temperature also increases drought in areas that receive little rain. Stronger storms elsewhere suck in the moisture that might otherwise cause occasional rain in arid regions. The persistent drought in the Sahel (the area just south of Africa's Sahara) is probably due to the inability of moisture to escape strong storms over the tropical Atlantic and over the northern Indian Ocean.

Chapter 6, Quiz 3 (page 128)

Investigating the Relationship of Biology to Emotion

Cultures tend to speak of a certain biological feature as the seat of emotion. In many European cultures, the heart is where love or sadness resides. In Malay-speaking cultures, the liver plays that role. In English, the spleen is blamed for vengefulness. Neverthless, such expressions do not express any current scientific view of reality, if they ever did. They are metaphors. No one believes that emotions really arise from one internal organ or another—except, perhaps, the brain.

Research on brain chemistry is showing ever more convincingly that many emotions and personality traits depend on the levels of certain chemicals in the brain and the degree to which they are absorbed. This research is independent of the famous experiments in which an electric current applied to a certain part of the brain causes the subject to "see" an imaginary butterfly or "hear" nonexistent music. The focus is on chemicals, both on the complex and poorly understood neurotransmitters like serotonin and on the balances of such prosaic elements as copper, calcium, and iron in the blood stream.

A single Dutch family offered clues that neurotransmitters might have a direct effect on such emotions as depression and aggression. Male members of that family, generation after generation, exhibited anomalously violent behavior. When DNA samples were taken from the still-living members of the family, a genetic sequence on the X chromosome of the males was found to trigger the excessive release of an enzyme called monoamine oxidase A. As a result, a class of drugs known as the monoamine oxidase inhibitors (MAOIs) are commonly prescribed for patients who have a tendency toward unexplained aggressiveness or frustration.

The story of serotonin is even more intriguing and ultimately profitable for pharmaceutical companies. Produced by the pineal gland at the base of the brain, serotonin helps relay messages from one nerve cell to another in the brain. Research on serotonin itself, which is not found in the blood, would require invasive and dangerous brain surgery. But researchers discovered an indirect serotonin-measurement technique.

Common forms of depression and anxiety occurred in patients who showed abnormally low levels of chemicals (called indicators) that decrease when serotonin levels decrease. This hinted at an overall low level of serotonin in the brains of such patients. By taking a selective serotonin reuptake inhibitor (SSRI) like Prozac® or Zoloft®, a patient can discourage excessive absorption of serotonin by the nerve cells. Each SSRI has its own chemical composition, and it may take a while for a doctor to find exactly the right SSRI for a particular patient. However, the high rate of effectiveness among SSRIs (greater than 50 percent, if the patient takes medication as scheduled) indicates that medical assumptions about a relationship between serotonin levels and emotional disorders are generally correct.

Chapter 7, Quiz 3 (page 146)

Analysts Ponder Factors in BelSync's Profitable Quarter

Since BelSync, Inc., reported record profits for the fourth quarter of last year, financial analysts have been asking themselves, "How did they do it?" Officers of the Greenville-based telecommunications giant aren't offering any clues. "Let's just say we have solved some problems that our competitors are still struggling with," said Chief Operations Officer Marisa Josephson. This hint of some powerful trade secret has only intensified speculation among stock analysts.

One theory involves some remarkably creative bargaining between BelSync and the union representing most of its employees, the International Union of Telephonists (IUT). On paper, the labor contract seems unremarkable. Any labor-related magic must lie in some informal understanding between the IUT and BelSync. Did the company offer profit-sharing in return for a promise of IUT docility? Perhaps.

Other explanations involve the departure of former CEO Mark Hawks, who resigned early last year for "personal reasons." James Sobel of IDC Analysts Group thinks there might have been other reasons. "Rumors of bribery, pressure on investment funds, and personal use of company money swirled around Hawks eighteen months ago. He was never formally accused of a crime, but his sudden departure may have been part of a deal to prevent a nasty, damaging trial."

Then again, on the more technical side, BelSync may like the way research is going on its "unhackable" wireless system. Skeptics point out that no system is unhackable, but BelSync's doesn't have to be perfect to make a big noise. If security can be pushed into the 80 percent range, the company can brag about a system at least 30 percent more secure than any competitor's. "To get any more unhackable than that with today's technology, you'd have to lock up every teenager and 20-something nerd in America," says IDC's Sobel.

Chapter 8, Quiz 3 (page 168)

Federal Power and States' Rights

The United States of America has a federal system of government, which means that smaller units (the states) have granted certain powers to the central government in Washington, DC — "the federal government." More than 200 years of debate have still not settled a fundamental issue: Where are the boundaries between federal power and states' rights?

The Revolutionary War was followed by nearly a decade of chaos under the very weak Articles of Confederation, which provided no effective central government at all. The new states somewhat reluctantly opted for more centralization by ratifying the U.S. Constitution. Many Americans remained suspicious of a central power, and ratification was anything but certain. In fact, when George Washington took office as president in 1789, only 9 of the original 13 states had ratified it.

Disagreements over the rights of states versus those of the federal government have caused some of the greatest conflicts in U.S. history. The Civil War of the 1860s was only partly about slavery. More fundamentally, it was about the federal imposition of tariffs (import fees) that disadvantaged most of the southern states, federal control of property (such as forts or naval docks) outside the District of Columbia, and other matters defining the federal-state relationship. Ultimately the southernmost states asserted the right to break away from the federation, a split that deeply troubled President Abraham Lincoln.

During the grim years of the Great Depression and World War II, federal action was generally more acceptable to Americans, largely because only a full-scale national effort could tackle the poverty, unemployment, and threat of foreign attack that prevailed at that time. Under President Franklin D. Roosevelt, federal programs like the Works Progress Administration and the Civilian Conservation Corps made large segments of the American workforce employees of the national government. Private businesses and state governments lacked the resources to help out-of-work Americans on any comparable scale.

The Civil Rights Movement in the 1950s and 1960s was fraught with federal-state conflict. One famous example is the showdown between Governor George Wallace of Alabama and President John F. Kennedy in June 1963. Wallace, who began his political career as a moderate on the issue of race relations, was anything but a moderate on states' rights. When the federal government ordered the state to integrate the University of Alabama at Birmingham, Wallace bitterly opposed it on the grounds that the federal government had no right to interfere in Alabama's educational institutions. Wallace stood in the doorway of the university's administration building as if to bar the entry of two African Americans who hoped to register. He stepped aside, however, as the two approached, accompanied by armed members of the Alabama National Guard. Kennedy had prevailed, largely because he had federalized the Alabama guard, requiring them to obey Kennedy's orders instead of, as usual, the governor's. It was a masterful stroke, ensuring that Wallace would have to confront home-grown Alabama guardsmen in order to defy federal power.

In the early 21st century, a somewhat contradictory political climate prevailed. The federal government was controlled by right-wing advocates of states' rights who nevertheless expanded the power of the federal government over the individual and the states. Washington issued sweeping federal mandates to the states and localities about a wide range of issues, from school performance to airport security, without providing enough federal money to fund the required changes. The Patriot Act of 2001 authorized large-scale federal surveillance of ordinary citizens. In 2005, the Congress authorized federal judges to rule about the medical treatment of an individual patient in a Florida hospital. In the following days, however, one federal judge after another refused to intervene in what they saw as a matter for the State of Florida to settle.

Chapter 9, Quiz 3 (page 187)

Some Defenses against Disease

A bacterial infection triggers several parts of the human immune system. The action of white blood cells is well known. They are part of the primary immune system.

A less-well-known component is called the complement system. It is composed of chemical enzymes and blood plasma. Sensing an infection, enzymes called permeability mediators cause the blood vessels to release fluids from the complement system so they can attack the invaders. Meanwhile, some varieties of phagocytes (eater cells) arrive at the site of the infection. They release proteins and other chemicals that burn holes in the invader cells.

At the same time, other parts of the immune system attack invaders with a variety of weapons.

A strong immune system is remarkably effective at defending the body even against the growth of some kinds of cancer. Unfortunately, the system can be weakened not only by certain viruses (such as Human Immunodeficiency Virus) but also by environmental factors like radiation or toxic chemicals. Some researchers theorize that this partly explains why residents of highly polluted areas have exceptionally high cancer rates. According to this scenario, industrial poisons don't actually cause the cancers but prevent the body from dealing with those that develop from other causes.

The great promise of DNA research is not really the linking of a certain disease to a certain gene or combination of genes. Gene therapy will work best if it can be made to strengthen the body's own defenses. Defense by the self is far preferable to external rescue. Manipulating genes to produce needed proteins—and, very importantly, to reproduce cells that can keep producing it—is the key technology. Anything else is just another way of administering chemical medicines, which falls far short of a permanent cure.

ANSWER KEY

Unit I

Essay Exercises (pages 8–11)

Hormone Production

Introduction

Endocrine disorders (malfunctions of the human hormone-producing mechanisms) can have serious consequences. Hormones, like insulin or human growth hormone, are crucial physical messengers, regulating and coordinating such functions as digestion and the balance of serum minerals. Severe shortages of hormones can mean a virtual shutdown of essential bodily processes.

Endocrine disorders are routinely treated by administering hormones obtained from sources outside the body of the person suffering the disorder. The supply of such chemicals in nature, however, is far short of that needed in modern medicine. Since hormones are proteins, they are perfect candidates for production by genetically engineered bacteria. This production represents one of the most useful and widespread applications of rDNA (recombinant DNA) technology.

Introduction paragraphs

Thesis statement

More than 5 million people worldwide take the hormone *insulin* each day to control some form of diabetes. Most of the insulin sold comes from cow or pig pancreases collected at abattoirs as a byproduct of meat production. While insulin from these sources is generally safe, it has slight structural differences from the human form. Rather than slipping comfortably past the immune defenses of the recipient, these insulin molecules are easily recognized as outsiders. Consequently, a few people taking bovine or porcine insulin develop allergic reactions as their immune systems reject the foreign intrusion. This problem is avoided by substituting human insulin, which, to be available in significant quantities, must be manufactured by genetically altered bacteria.

— Topic sentence

— Supporting idea

Insulin was the first therapeutic rDNA product approved by the FDA for sale in the United States. It went on the market in 1982 under the brand name Humulin®. The development work had been done by the pioneering biotech firm Genentech; Eli Lilly and Company produced and marketed Humulin®.

— Topic sentence

— Supporting idea

The biotechnology used in making insulin is more complicated than that used in making human growth hormone. The insulin molecule is made up of two polypeptide chains (linked strings of amino acids), which join to make the active form of insulin. In the production of genetically engineered insulin, the DNA that codes for the A chain is introduced into one batch of *E. coli* bacteria and the DNA for the B chain into a different one. The bacterial cells are induced to make the two chains, which are then collected, mixed, and chemically treated to make them link. The resulting insulin molecules are identical to those secreted by the human pancreas.

— Topic sentence

— Supporting ideas

Human growth hormone (hGH) was another early target of rDNA approaches to hormone deficiency. HGH controls the growth of bones and regulates weight

— Topic sentence

gain. In some children, the pituitary gland fails to produce enough hGH for normal development, and this is — *Supporting ideas*
evidenced by markedly short stature (perhaps only 60%–70% of normal height for a given age) and other growth deficiencies. The condition can be ameliorated, but only if hormone supplementation takes place during the growth years of childhood. Beyond this critical period, many bones (such as the femur) lose their ability to elongate.

Early in the development of hGH therapy, the only — *Topic sentence*
sources of the hormone were the pituitary glands of human cadavers. Suppliers and marketers worried that drawing a chemical from the glands of the dead might eventually create a public relations problem. But a more serious problem was that the source was not prolific enough. First of all, the number of cadavers from which the pituitary gland could be harvested was very limited and not easily increased (within the bounds of the law). — *Supporting ideas*
Secondly, each cadaver yielded a very small amount of the hormone—only about 4 mg, whereas one week's treatment for an individual deficient in hGH requires about 7 mg. No successful animal sources were found. Clearly, new sources were needed.

The supply of human growth hormone is maintained — *Topic sentence*
by applying rDNA techniques and achieving high-volume synthesis. A gene for hGH production is spliced — *Supporting idea*
into *E. coli*, which are cultured and exploited in very large amounts. A 500-liter tank of bacterial culture can } *Concluding paragraph*
produce as much hGH as could have been derived from 35,000 cadavers. Growth hormone produced by this technique was approved for human use in 1985 and is now commonplace.

Source: Adapted from Cynthia S. Gross, *The New Biotechnology: Putting Microbes to Work* (Minneapolis: Lerner, 1988).

Exercise: Choosing the Best Thesis Statement *(page 12)*

Page 21 in *Building Academic Vocabulary,* Writing Project 2. The following are some sentences people might try to use as a thesis statement for an essay about this question. Which ones are the best, and why?

Recommended ranking:

1. According to *Webster's Ninth New Collegiate Dictionary*, a family is "a group of individuals living under one roof and usually under one head."

2. Throughout the world, there are many different kinds of families, so it is impossible to say exactly what a family is.

3. In order to meet the needs of the sick, the poor, and other unfortunates, it is best to think of the family as an extended group involving three or four generations—from great-grandparents to young children.

Exercise: Topic Sentences *(page 13)*

1. The invention of the laser makes for a somewhat unclear chapter in technological history.

2. Since the 19th century, cultural diffusionists have explained shared features among various cultures in terms of a process of contact and borrowing.

3. Superconductivity requires certain conditions of temperature, current density, and magnetic field strength. These create important changes in the arrangement of molecules within a material.

4. **Possible answer:** Not many teachers would feel comfortable showing it to their students.

5. **Possible answer:** It is clear that Earth's climate can be affected by the level of sunspot activity.

Unit 2

Chapter 1 (pages 21–38)

Additional Vocabulary Quiz *(page 23)*

I. **Categorizing (page 3)**

   1. superficial

   2. autopsy

   3. compass

   4. shores

   5. arthritis

II. **Paraphrasing (page 24)**

   Answers will vary. Some possible paraphrases:

   1. The great thing about e-mail is that it cuts down on time-consuming conversations.

   2. The average commute for people in the Twin Cities metro area is 45 minutes one way.

   3. Only four people have access to the safe.

   4. Houston, Texas, is the nucleus of the Green Environmental Board.

   5. Planes measure wind speed and air pressure by flying into the center of a hurricane.

Quiz 1 *(page 26)*

I. **Fill in the Blanks (page 26)**

   1. All told

   2. made up of

   3. involves

   4. contains

   5. constitute

II. Paraphrasing (page 27)

Answers will vary. Some possible paraphrases:

1. Most scientific theories started out as ideas far from the mainstream.

2. The Oort Cloud, an area of space just outside our solar system, is composed of a relatively dense center and an immense region of widely dispersed icy particles.

3. The term *the tropics* technically encompasses all locations between 23° north latitude and 23° south latitude.

4. Most tree trunks consist of several rings of woody xylem on the inside and a surrounding layer of phloem, including the bark, on the outside.

5. Becoming a licensed psychiatrist is not easy because it involves having to complete medical school and get a psychology degree.

Quiz 2 *(page 29)*

I. Sentence Completion (page 29)

1. comprehensive

2. form

3. comprises

4. make up

5. encompasses (see "Usage Clues," *BAV,* p. 7)

II. Paraphrasing (page 30)

Answers will vary. Some possible paraphrases:

1. Currently, the U.S. military is composed entirely of volunteers. There are no draftees at this time.

2. The agricultural approach known as the Green Revolution encompassed a variety of techniques, from the development of hardier seeds to more efficient ways of plowing the soil.

3. If we want to avoid unpleasant confrontations, we should make sure that the guest list for the party does not include both Gordon and Pete.

4. Getting a scholarship to Charles University involves filling out two application forms, writing an essay, presenting a portfolio of your achievements, and speaking personally with four or five administrators.

5. A time capsule is a sealed box or tube that contains items common in everyday life at the time the capsule is filled.

Quiz 3 *(page 32)*

I. Collocations and Common Phrases (page 32)

1. a wide range of

2. investigation

3. total

4. decided to

5. dangerous attempts

6. bomb

7. into

8. of

II. Paraphrasing (page 33)

Answers will vary. Some possible paraphrases:

1. The Akrubian calendar comprised five seasons: the dry cold, the wet cold, the planting time, the heat, and the harvest.

2. The accounting department is made up of the accounts receivable, accounts payable, tax accounting, and general ledger divisions.

3. If you include students on our bowling team, table tennis team, and cheerleading squad, all told, 213 students at Ford High School play some sort of varsity sport.

4. Antarctica consists of the continental landmass, nearby ice shelves, ice-filled seas, and islands south of about 70 south latitude.

5. The public transit system in the Twin Cities is composed of bus routes and one new light-rail line from downtown Minneapolis to the airport.

Quiz 4 *(page 35)*

I. Fill in the Blanks (page 35)

1. evolution
2. compass
3. component
4. content
5. contents

II. Paraphrasing (page 36)

Answers will vary. Some possible paraphrases:

1. The teller carefully counted my money and confirmed that I was depositing $750.
2. Many people are surprised to learn that the Earth's atmosphere consists primarily of nitrogen.
3. You have to give each question a comprehensive treatment to get an A on your term paper.
4. Charles Darwin espoused a Theory of Natural Selection. Later interpreters started incorrectly calling it the Theory of Evolution.
5. Since school facilities are used for our meetings, the chess club should be inclusive of all the students at the school.

Chapter 2 (pages 39–57)

Additional Vocabulary Quiz 1 *(page 41)*

I. Categorizing (page 41)

1. contract
2. tumor
3. poll
4. illegible
5. an appealing idea

II. Paraphrasing (page 42)

Answers will vary. Some possible paraphrases:

1. Fingerprints found at the scene of the crime were the strongest evidence against Jackson.

2. The press followed the Princess of Wales everywhere.

3. Heather showed her strong character by remaining calm while her roommates got upset.

4. Some very talented graphic designers work for the Corey Jones advertising company.

5. Bart's response to my e-mail was long overdue.

Quiz 1 *(page 44)*

I. Fill in the Blanks (page 44)

1. exclude

2. bans

3. rogue

4. egregious

5. marginal

6. filter

II. Paraphrasing (page 45)

Answers will vary. Some possible paraphrases:

1. The police academy carefully screens applicants to detect anyone who might have an unhealthy desire to use violence against suspects.

2. Ellie felt like an outcast in her neighborhood.

3. With the exception of the green patches on the skin, almost every part of a raw potato is edible.

4. The practice of calling one's parents by their first names is alien to me.

5. Monotremes are anomalous among other mammals in that they lay eggs instead of giving birth to live young.

Quiz 2 *(page 48)*

I. Sentence Completion (page 48)

1. excluded

2. marginal

3. screens

4. outcast

5. banned

II. Paraphrasing (page 48)

Answers will vary. Some possible paraphrases:

1. Until Europeans began settling in Australia, its remote location kept out the animals of other continents.

2. I usually drive faster than the speed limit, but I try not to be egregious about it so the police don't notice me.

3. An anomalous dark patch (called the black-drop effect) distorts the outline of the planet Venus when it appears to cross the sun (a transit of Venus).

4. A rogue soldier broke away from his unit and started shooting, even though the commander had ordered all troops to stay where they were and not fire.

5. You can buy inexpensive software to filter spam out of your e-mail messages.

6. By embedding reporters with troop units in Iraq, the U.S. military carefully screens bad news from what is reported to the public.

Quiz 3 *(page 51)*

I. Collocations and Common Phrases (page 51)

1. through

2. among, in that

3. sole

4. out

5. inalienable rights

6. social

7. from

8. state

9. out

II. Paraphrasing (page 52)

Answers will vary. Some possible paraphrases:

1. The Alpha Tau fraternity is so exclusive that even the governor's son was not allowed to join.

2. Because citizens of Nejd-Nafar can easily buy and hide satellite dishes, the government can't keep foreign ideas out of the kingdom.

3. Jenna Peavey didn't really love Timmy Lee. She was just intrigued by the chance to change an outcast into an acceptable person.

4. The electron telescopes on Mt. Taylor were picking up an anomalous radiation signal from a seemingly empty part of the galaxy.

5. The school board banned any discussion of its meeting with anyone who wasn't present.

Quiz 4 (page 54)

I. Fill in the Blanks (page 54)

1. cast, out

2. exclusive

3. marginalized

4. screening

5. anomaly

II. Paraphrasing (page 55)

Answers will vary. Some possible paraphrases:

1. The Borenalian prime minister accused Feringistan of being an arrogant rogue state.

2. Liquirhine, a new decongestant, was approved for all patients, with the sole exception of those who have had inner-ear problems.

3. The city decided to tear down old, uninhabited buildings, excluding historically protected structures.

4. The U.S. Declaration of Independence spoke of certain inalienable rights—life, liberty, and the pursuit of happiness.

5. The governor was embarrassed by her brother's egregious behavior, such as his dancing on the tables at the inaugural ball.

Unit 3

Chapter 3 (pages 59–76)

Additional Vocabulary Quiz (page 61)

I. Categorizing (page 61)

1. glacier

2. defer to

3. environmental

4. reggae

5. natural resources

II. Paraphrasing (page 62)

Answers will vary. Some possible paraphrases:

1. Even though I don't agree with my lawyer's decisions, I defer to her superior knowledge of how the courts work.

2. If you set up a computer network in your home, make sure you can easily add to your equipment in the future.

3. The plants in the office withered during the holidays since no one watered them.

4. Because of a lack of rain, large parts of Africa suffered from several periods of famine in the late 20th century.

5. The United States briefly enacted Prohibition in the 1920s.

Quiz 1 *(page 64)*

I. Fill in the Blanks (page 64)

1. parallel

2. alike

3. clone

4. Just as

5. image

6. echoes (*or* echoed)

II. Paraphrasing (page 65)

Answers will vary. Some possible paraphrases:

1. If a 40-year prison sentence is the penalty for possessing a small amount of drugs, there is no parity between the seriousness of the crime and the harshness of the punishment.

2. Because plants can pollinate themselves, the genetic make-up of an offspring can be identical to that of its one parent.

3. The professional convention gave Jane a chance to meet her counterparts from other companies.

4. The state of Vermont banned the importation of trash for burial there. The State of Minnesota did likewise.

5. If we want to ensure equality in access to computer services, we have to set up labs throughout the campus.

Quiz 2 *(page 67)*

I. Sentence Completion (page 67)

1. identical

2. image

3. equivalent

4. counterpart

5. parity (*Equality* is also possible, but *parity* is better because the context implies a standard.)

II. Paraphrasing (page 68)

Answers will vary. Some possible paraphrases:

1. Recent steep increases in United States housing prices echo those in Japan during the early 1990s.

2. The teachers and students alike denounced the new dress-code policy.

3. A U.S. university curriculum in nuclear physics is parallel to those at most European universities.

4. Verro Appliance Co. is trying to achieve market-share parity with its competitors.

5. Joe is applying to medical schools, and Al is under pressure from his mom to do likewise.

Quiz 3 (page 70)

I. Collocations and Common Phrases (page 70)

1. division

2. her

3. in

4. virtually

5. routes

6. achieve

7. in that

8. combination

II. Paraphrasing (page 71)

Answers will vary. Some possible paraphrases:

1. Members of Congress have a responsibility to respect the American consensus that all citizens should be treated with equality.

2. The planets Mercury and Venus sometimes exhibit retrograde motion, an apparent backward course across the night sky. Mars does likewise.

3. People hoping to be distinctive in their fashionable clothing often end up looking like clones of each other.

4. Just as the students were shocked by the principal's decision to cancel all field trips, so were the teachers.

5. The Korean and Japanese languages alike use some syllable-based sets of characters in their writing systems.

Quiz 4 *(page 73)*

I. Fill in the Blanks (page 73)

1. like

2. echo

3. equivalence

4. identity

5. parallels

6. cloning

II. Paraphrasing (page 74)

Answers will vary. Some possible paraphrases:

1. Through the Sister Cities program, our mayor got to meet her counterpart from Sendai, Japan.

2. The candidates for the job were equally qualified.

3. The average worker in Costa Brava earns the equivalent of about US$30.

4. In her wedding dress, Marlene is the very image of her grandmother.

5. Alec's doctoral studies in England paralleled Harvey's at the University of Arizona.

Chapter 4 (pages 77–94)

Additional Vocabulary Quiz (page 79)

I. Categorizing (page 79)

1. infrastructure
2. auditor
3. massive
4. immoral
5. portfolio

II. Paraphrasing (page 80)

Answers will vary. Some possible paraphrases:

1. Adequate security in school buildings involves not just protection from threats, but also attending to an emergency once it has started.
2. I just don't have time to respond to every problem expressed by members of our staff.
3. Many musicians can learn the guitar well enough to have some fun with it, but very few are able to actually make a career of it.
4. Investors who plan for the long term are not impressed by a boom in things like real estate or Internet-related stocks.
5. It's a good idea to dig a shallow trench around the base of your tent. Otherwise, heavy rains will flow under the tent.

Quiz 1 (page 82)

I. Fill in the Blanks (page 82)

1. disparity
2. disparate
3. discrete
4. inequality
5. contrasts
6. differentiate

II. Paraphrasing (page 83)

Answers will vary. Some possible paraphrases:

1. The population of America is heterogeneous.

2. One word may have many meanings; only by looking at the context can one distinguish between those meanings.

3. Students study English as a Foreign Language for diverse purposes.

4. The views expressed by Senators Burton and Craft about environmental laws diverged during the last election campaign.

5. There was a discrepancy between her performance on the final test and the rest of her grades from the semester.

Quiz 2 *(page 85)*

I. Sentence Completion (page 85)

1. diverse

2. discrete

3. contrast

4. heterogeneous

5. differ

II. Paraphrasing (page 86)

Answers will vary. Some possible paraphrases:

1. In many countries, men and women experience almost no inequality in job opportunities.

2. John believes that his university degree, a Masters in Business Administration, will distinguish him from other job applicants.

3. A great disparity in wealth could lead to political instability in newly prosperous countries.

4. The president's view of the university's mission has diverged greatly from that of most professors.

5. The two families share religious beliefs, but they differ on what their children should be allowed to do.

6. A line of stem cells comprises several generations of versatile cells that have not yet differentiated into specific cells for body parts.

Quiz 3 *(page 89)*

I. Collocations and Common Phrases (page 89)

1. from
2. between
3. investments
4. significant (*or* stark)
5. population
6. parts
7. intervals
8. stark
9. candidates
10. drops

II. Paraphrasing (page 90)

Answers will vary. Some possible paraphrases:

1. The time has come for us to fight against inequality in the treatment of people because of race, gender, or social class.
2. Even though her ideas differ from the committee's recommendations, they are still quite good and should be considered.
3. One sociologist found that after ten years of marriage, women's views had diverged from those of their husbands.
4. Debt distinguishes the present sluggishness in the economy from that of ten years ago.
5. A reporter on National Public Radio claimed that there was a disparity between the wages paid to women and to men for the same work.

Quiz 4 *(page 92)*

I. Fill in the Blanks (page 92)

1. diverse
2. contrast
3. distinguish

4. diverge

5. discrete

II. Paraphrasing (page 93)

Answers will vary. Some possible paraphrases:

1. The committee could not reach an agreement. There was a great disparity among Susan's, Jeff's, and Jill's ideas about ticket prices.

2. Phil and Chris take disparate approaches to managing their businesses.

3. An infant separated from his or her mother can suffer a severe emotional shock, since the infant does not fully differentiate between himself or herself and the mother.

4. Some people differ on when to fly their flags at half mast: when a public servant or soldier dies or when any notable person passes away.

5. Inequality in voting rights between men and women is still an issue in many countries.

Chapter 5 (pages 95–111)

Additional Vocabulary Quiz (page 97)

I. Categorizing (page 97)

1. consensus

2. militant

3. veteran

4. scandal

5. fuel-efficient

II. Paraphrasing (page 98)

Answers will vary. Some possible paraphrases:

1. Along with a high fever, Carl had severe muscle aches and fatigue.

2. Ms. Terrell had to resign from her job because of a scandal over improper hiring practices.

3. Cars that run on diesel fuel generally get better mileage than cars that run on gasoline.

4. There is a general consensus in our state that mature forests should not be cut down to make way for development.

5. The renovation of the stadium had to be postponed for financial reasons.

Quiz 1 *(page 100)*

I. Fill in the Blanks (page 100)

1. expand
2. declined
3. modify
4. accelerate
5. transform
6. contract

II. Paraphrasing (page 101)

Answers will vary. Some possible paraphrases:

1. The Ridgeline Association hoped to raise awareness of the local deforestation problem.
2. Working in the refugee camps transformed Beth.
3. The Internet has reduced the amount of time we wait to correspond with someone.
4. The magazine will be redesigned to expand its audience.
5. In the years following the Cold War, the army of the Soviet Union gradually diminished in size.

Quiz 2 *(page 103)*

I. Sentence Completion (page 103)

1. restructure
2. rise
3. transition
4. expand
5. diminish

II. Paraphrasing (page 104)

Answers will vary. Some possible paraphrases:

1. Some senators altered the proposed law so it could more easily be approved by the senate as a whole.

2. In order for the company to expand, it must search for more new clients.

3. As gas prices declined, more people began to buy bigger cars and travel more on the highways.

4. The two governments hope to accelerate the progress of peace in the region.

5. Einstein's laws of relativity proposed that under the right conditions time can dilate and space can contract.

Quiz 3 (page 106)

I. Collocations and Common Phrases (page 106)

1. from, into
2. development
3. plants
4. behavior
5. in
5. course
7. equally
8. of
9. treatment
10. influence

II. Paraphrasing (page 107)

Answers will vary. Some possible paraphrases:

1. The couple is going through a time of transition as their children go to college and they move to a new city.

2. Teacher-training institutes must redesign their credential programs to include professional development credits.

3. New regulations have forced the company to restructure its benefits plan.

4. Many senators support new legislation that will restrict immigration.

5. During a heartbeat, the ventricles contract, pushing blood out of the heart into large blood vessels.

Quiz 4 *(page 109)*

I. Fill in the Blanks (page 109)

1. expand

2. transform

3. raised

4. alter

5. rises

II. Paraphrasing (page 110)

Answers will vary. Some possible paraphrases:

1. In extreme heat or cold, the spider's egg sack contracts to only about one-half its normal size.

2. Many students take evening English-pronunciation classes to reduce their accents.

3. As book printing became more reliant on electronic equipment, printers and publishers had to restructure their production departments.

4. You should modify your presentation to Mr. DeFord, who is well known for letting religion influence his business decisions.

5. Through the middle to late 1990s, the number of hurricanes striking Florida declined.

Unit 4

Chapter 6 (pages 113–32)

Additional Vocabulary Quiz *(page 115)*

I. Categorizing (page 115)

1. algae

2. freckle

3. lactase

4. baldness

5. wage

II. Paraphrasing (page 116)

Answers will vary. Some possible paraphrases:

1. China has only one time zone, from Urumqi in the far west to Shanghai on the east coast.

2. Many movies directed by John Hughes are set in affluent suburbs north and northwest of Chicago.

3. To pull a car out of a ditch, you need a big truck and a chain to link the car to the truck.

4. The spread of vine-borers can only be stopped by killing the insects before they enter adulthood.

5. The dean emphasized that attendance at the meeting was not optional.

Quiz 1 *(page 119)*

I. Fill in the Blanks (page 119)

1. imply

2. accompany

3. infer

4. characteristic of

5. goes along with

6. correlation

II. Paraphrasing (page 120)

Answers will vary. Some possible paraphrases:

1. The combination of rough natural materials, such as fieldstone, with smooth, clear-finished wood and broad expanses of glass is characteristic of Prairie Style architecture.

2. Numerous surveys have shown that, everything else being equal, a college degree is associated with earnings about twice as high as those available with only a high school diploma.

3. Scientists have long known there is a link between obesity and diabetes.

4. Advertising is more effective if ads in print media are run in conjunction with television commercials taking a similar approach.

5. To the degree that a nation's per capita income rises, its divorce rate will rise.

Quiz 2 *(page 122)*

I. Sentence Completion (page 122)

1. associated with

2. to the degree that

3. imply

4. goes along with

5. linked to

II. Paraphrasing (page 123)

Answers will vary. Some possible paraphrases:

1. New studies show a correlation between the ease of voter registration and the number of people who actually vote.

2. The development of new species often accompanies the isolation of animals and plants.

3. Speaking honestly to others is characteristic of most successful managers.

4. The Casnovian Philosophical Society will have its annual meeting in conjunction with that of its parent organization, the North American Philosophical Society.

5. To me a huge amount of money in a politician's campaign fund implies dishonesty and corruption.

Quiz 3 *(page 126)*

I. Collocations and Common Phrases (page 126)

1. positive

2. mutual respect

3. to

4. meanings

5. risk

6. side effects

7. with

8. is, of

9. are, with

II. Paraphrasing (page 127)

Answers will vary. Some possible paraphrases:

1. There was a link between a tuberculosis epidemic and the worldwide spread of Human Immunodeficiency Virus (HIV).

2. From the pattern of plant growth along the dunes, we can infer that a strong, steady northwest wind blows off the lake.

3. The placing of great value on the ownership of cattle in an east African society implies some Bantu influence on that society.

4. The dreaded plague that swept Europe in the Middle Ages was called the bubonic plague because of the buboes—inflammations of the lymph nodes—that accompanied the disease.

5. There is a correlation between the size of the company and the salary of its senior executives.

Quiz 4 *(page 129)*

I. Fill in the Blanks (page 129)

1. went along with

2. characterized

3. associate

4. to the degree that

5. implicit

II. Paraphrasing (page 130)

Answers will vary. Some possible paraphrases:

1. From a male's coloration, female birds apparently draw an inference about his ability to breed successfully.

2. According to Professor Ghazal's astrophysical research, the strength of a star's "stellar wind" is a correlative of its age.

3. Oncologists have linked intestinal cancer to such personality traits as excessive worrying.

4. According to Professor Thorvald's work from the 1970s, being female is one implication of being a feminist.

5. The United Nations report focused on economic diversity in seven countries and their accompanying economic stability.

Chapter 7 (pages 133–51)

Additional Vocabulary Quiz (page 135)

I. Categorizing (page 135)

1. opaque
2. funding
3. speechless
4. slash-and-burn
5. colonialism

II. Paraphrasing (page 136)

Answers will vary. Some possible paraphrases:

1. To get good airflow in a room, you should open at least two windows—one across the room from the other.

2. No matter what I have to sacrifice, I will make sure my children get a good education.

3. Because security was lax, thieves got into the building and stole three valuable works of art.

4. Mr. Trent is the senior worker on the staff.

5. Flight 841 was delayed by bad weather.

Quiz 1 *(page 138)*

I. Fill in the Blanks (page 138)

1. promote

2. are responsible for

3. generates

4. provoke

5. stem from

II. Paraphrasing (page 139)

Answers will vary. Some possible paraphrases:

1. After Jim Stadler lost the election for county commissioner, he claimed that local television stations had favored his opponent.

2. Stock market analysts have predicted that software companies will generate greater profits next year than in other recent years.

3. Modern misunderstanding of silent films from the early 20th century derives from the fact that many visual symbols of that era have lost their meaning.

4. On July 12, 1965, a leak from a chemical tank led to the death of 73 people in Monakwah Valley.

5. The governor argued that his advisors should be blamed for his mistakes.

Quiz 2 *(page 141)*

I. Sentence Completion (page 141)

1. render

2. made

3. are due to

4. yield

5. generating

II. Paraphrasing (page 142)

Answers will vary. Some possible paraphrases:

1. Sucralose, though about 600 times sweeter than sugar, does not promote tooth decay.

2. Even very small errors in the measurement of current weather conditions can render weather forecasts undependable.

3. His timidity didn't stem from an unwillingness to express himself but from painful embarrassment over his speech problems.

4. Richard's painful divorce generated distrust between his family and his ex-wife's.

5. The weather on the eastern seaboard favors kite-flying, especially when onshore winds are brisk but not too strong.

Quiz 3 (page 144)

I. Collocations and Common Phrases (page 144)

1. income
2. resentment
3. jealousy
4. development
5. to
6. tends to
7. from
8. primarily
9. has been
10. in

II. Paraphrase (page 145)

Answers will vary. Some possible paraphrases:

1. The Senator hopes that a visit to his home state will lead to a better understanding of his constituents' real needs so he can better represent them in Washington.

2. The $1 million fines levied against Arthur Jones stem from his conviction for illegally altering the financial records of his trucking business.

3. The manager deliberately provoked the employees to strike.

4. Anomalies in magnetic pressure, gas pressure, and gas temperature are probably due to the formation of sunspots.

5. The Khmer Rouge government is responsible for the death of more than a million Cambodians in the 1970s.

Quiz 4 *(page 147)*

I. Fill in the Blanks (page 147)

1. derives from

2. render

3. were responsible for

4. provoked

5. favors

II. Paraphrasing (page 148)

Answers will vary. Some possible paraphrases:

1. The teacher believed that the new textbook would not yield very good results for most students.

2. An increase in the recruiting budget should help promote diversity among the university's student body.

3. A defective engine part called an O-ring can almost certainly be blamed for the space-shuttle disaster.

4. A steady rise in the average height of the population in Tejatria is probably due to better nourishment.

5. Made-for-TV movies generate a lot of profits for television companies because their production costs are relatively low.

Chapter 8 (pages 153–71)

Additional Vocabulary Quiz (page 155)

I. Categorizing (page 155)

1. transition

2. enforce

3. evaporation

4. upbringing

5. criticize

II. Paraphrasing (page 156)

Answers will vary. Some possible paraphrases:

1. Bezickas Construction Co. is looking for new equipment to help cut costs in building houses.

2. His upbringing in a small southern town trained him to address everyone as sir or ma'am.

3. Small businesses have to be very lucky to survive in a market economy.

4. We will interview the mayor at 4:00 tomorrow afternoon.

5. We have a problem with cash flow because customers have been so late in paying us.

Quiz 1 (page 158)

I. Fill in the Blanks (page 158)

1. facilitates

2. excuse

3. permit

4. ease

5. lenient

II. Paraphrasing (page 159)

Answers will vary. Some possible paraphrases:

1. Diet pills made from herbs are sold without the approval of the Food and Drug Administration.

2. The governor wrongly assumed that her re-election cleared the way for her to pursue whatever policies she liked.

3. The riders stopped at several grassy spots on the dry plateau to allow their horses to graze.

4. U.S. citizens who live in a foreign country and meet certain other requirements are exempt from paying U.S. income taxes.

5. Without the consent of the U.S. Senate, no presidential nominee can be appointed to the Supreme Court.

Quiz 2 *(page 162)*

I. Sentence Completion (page 162)

1. permit

2. remove obstacles to

3. allow

4. lenient

5. exempt from

II. Paraphrasing (page 163)

Answers will vary. Some possible paraphrases:

1. Reforming the Republic of Batang's international trading practices would facilitate the process of making high-quality foreign consumer goods more affordable.

2. After a lengthy period of fasting (choosing to eat or drink very little), sudden resumption of a solid-food diet is a painful mistake. Drinking only juices for a while can help ease the return to a solid-food diet.

3. The top two tennis players in the world would not permit authorities to conduct drug testing and were denied places in this weekend's Bellwood Invitational Tournament.

4. Prisoners who could provide guards with valuable information got more lenient treatment than most.

5. Even people who feel alienated from mainstream society feel a sense of belonging if they get the approval of other outcasts.

Quiz 3 *(page 166)*

I. Collocations and Common Phrases (page 166)

1. time
2. under
3. from
4. treated
5. give
6. get
7. be
8. herself
9. diagnosis
10. suffering

II. Paraphrasing (page 167)

Answers will vary. Some possible paraphrases:

1. Several religions do not allow men and women to worship in the same place.

2. The corps commander gave his consent for a tank battalion to race up the river valley toward the airport.

3. Because Galbraith has to take his child to the hospital, he will be excused from today's training session.

4. Parenting practices that seem normal to one family might seem very permissive to another.

5. The new proposal would exempt logging companies from long-standing bans on any vehicle traffic through national forests.

Quiz 4 *(page 169)*

I. Fill in the Blanks (page 169)

1. permits

2. consented

3. exemption

4. allowance

5. excuse

II. Paraphrasing (page 170)

Answers will vary. Some possible paraphrases:

1. Retaking the test and getting a higher score would remove a barrier to Simon's acceptance into Zwingli University.

2. The government should not interfere in the romantic relationship of two consenting adults.

3. The document isn't legal without your John Hancock.

4. Anyone who tries to predict future prices has to make allowances for inflation, which is a general tendency for prices to rise.

5. I'm willing to serve as a facilitator for you and your brother to discuss your differences, but I am not going to take any position about who's right and who's wrong.

Chapter 9 (pages 173–90)

Additional Vocabulary Quiz *(page 175)*

I. Categorizing (page 175)

1. drug-trafficking

2. injury

3. patrol

4. amnesty

5. swift

II. Paraphrasing (page 176)

Answers will vary. Some possible paraphrases:

1. My homework is overdue.

2. As the storm knocked down trees and power lines, the sheriff issued an appeal for everyone to stay indoors.

3. Jamie is a very talented writer, but she doesn't work hard at developing her abilities.

4. Attention, everyone. Let's get the meeting under way.

5. Earthquakes that send horizontal waves through soft soil cause more buildings to collapse than other types of earthquakes.

Quiz 1 (page 178)

I. Fill in the Blanks (page 178)

1. prevent

2. deny

3. blocks

4. hinder

5. restrict

6. suspended

II. Paraphrasing (page 179)

Answers will vary. Some possible paraphrases:

1. My religion forbids smoking and dancing.

2. Economic development in Barriaville is restrained by a very poor road system and undependable electric power.

3. The best way to deter bullies from bothering you is to have a lot of friends who will support you.

4. The referee halted the game because of a storm with frequent lightning.

5. My devotion to my family will never cease.

Quiz 2 *(page 182)*

I. Sentence Completion (page 182)

1. hinder

2. cease

3. forestall

4. halt

5. restrain

II. Paraphrasing (page 183)

Answers will vary. Some possible paraphrases:

1. In the United States, no-cost medical treatment is restricted to extremely poor people in emergency situations.

2. The Democratic Party tried hard to bring the bill to the Senate for a vote, but Senator Sterns successfully blocked it.

3. Most countries forbid the importation by visitors of fruits or vegetables from other countries.

4. To get information from the prisoners, soldiers would deny them water, food, and sleep.

5. Olympic gymnast Leva Fedova would not let a cold or fever deter her from competing.

Quiz 3 *(page 185)*

I. Collocations and Common Phrases (page 185)

1. to

2. are, to

3. from

4. in

5. from, getting

6. desist

7. call, to

8. indefinitely

9. myself

10. the invasion

II. Paraphrasing (page 186)

Answers will vary. Some possible paraphrases:

1. Because so many people are going out of town for the holiday, we should suspend rehearsals until mid-January.

2. I close my office door because the loud chatter from some colleagues hinders my work.

3. I don't really want my daughter to spend time with Jason, but I don't know how to prevent it without alienating her.

4. The library restricts the number of CDs you can take out at one time to three.

5. Because we got a huge new order, the management of our factory denied all requests for vacation from May 12 to May 30.

Quiz 4 *(page 188)*

I. Fill in the Blanks (page 188)

1. denial

2. restraints

3. cease

4. restriction

5. forbidden

II. Paraphrasing (page 189)

Answers will vary. Some possible paraphrases:

1. Some hydrologists say there's no way to forestall the complete drying up of the Aral Sea.

2. I was kept awake all night by the ceaseless barking of a neighbor's dog.

3. For some girls, going to an all-girl high school removes a hindrance to their studies.

4. Fantasy movies can work well if the audience achieves a suspension of disbelief.

5. For many years, the United States has relied on the deterrent effect of its nuclear weapons.